Green Energy for a Billion Poor

How Grameen Shakti Created a Winning Model for Social Business

Nancy Wimmer

Published by MCRE Verlag UG (haftungsbeschränkt)
www.mcreverlag.de

Cover design   Thomas W. Heffron
Copy editing   Kelli Christiansen
Photos   Subrin Al Azad, Grameen Shakti, Nancy Wimmer

For Klaus and Stephanie Ann

A technician installing a solar panel on the roof of a village house

Preface

Often the best alternative for expressing what one knows about the world is not an equation but a narrative – a story with real characters facing some kind of dilemma.
Thomas McCraw

A popular saying goes like this: when something is new, it is attacked as unrealistic. When later people admit this new thing is meeting with success, it is said to be unimportant. Finally, when its importance cannot be denied, people say, 'okay, but it's not new'.

This was my experience when introducing the business innovation *banking for the poor* to a European audience in the 1990s. When I first learned about the Grameen Bank and microcredit for the poor, a *bank for the poor* seemed exotic and unrealistic even to me. But I wanted to understand what made it work. My experience began in the villages of Bangladesh and continued in Nepal and India and later in Honduras, El Salvador, Egypt and Peru. I witnessed how tiny loans to poor women helped them generate a steady income and invest in their families' future. And I learned what counted most to understand: exposure to village life and hands-on experience.

When I came to know Grameen Shakti in 1996, I again witnessed an approach I had never encountered before—a company pioneering a new kind of energy business in one of the toughest business environments in the world: rural Bangladesh. I had studied projects geared to rural electrification in many countries, but Shakti was succeeding where many had failed. But why?

To understand how Shakti works challenged me to study its operations in the villages where it does business. On my many trips to the rural hinterland I experienced the work of Shakti's pioneering engineers, managers and staff; I learned from its village customers. I attended managers' meetings in Dhaka and learned about the many facets of running a highly decentralized rural company. But most of all, I learned how Shakti masters the art of rural business through social innovation and entrepreneurship.

This book reveals the story of Grameen Shakti, uncovering its remarkable growth, its pioneering philosophy and its entrepreneurial approach to business. It was a challenge to write. How should I describe a renewable energy service company which excels in an unpredictable rural environment? I use statistical data, facts collected from the field, rules and principles wherever possible. But I also convey intangibles: personal initiative, values, the will to spur economic growth in a poor country, the rewards of teamwork and a good sense of humor. I do this by telling the authentic stories of those who made Shakti happen, real-life narratives to relate what worked and what didn't.

Green Energy for a Billion Poor is a provocative but appropriate title. It highlights possibilities in the untapped market of a billion rural customers in developing countries who are deprived of electricity. It was written to make readers think of the need for entrepreneurial companies in a tough rural market. By the time this book is published, Grameen Shakti will have installed a million solar home systems to the benefit of millions of villagers in Bangladesh. It's possible. Shakti's successful model can be replicated, adapted, extended. If this happened, it would be the best reward for writing this book.

Nancy Wimmer

Acknowledgements

Special thanks for his vision, trust and long-time support go to Marcel Brenninkmeijer, Good Energies Foundation.

For their invaluable contributions during the process of publishing this book, I thank Dr. Clair Myers, Dr. Christian Schütze and Richenda Van Leeuwen.

I am much obliged to all who have facilitated and added to my stays in Bangladesh, in particular Azadul Haque, Dr. Alam Zahirul, and their kind families.

I thank the Acting Managing Director, Abser Kamal, and the Board of Grameen Shakti Social Business for supporting my work. Numerous experts and managers have shared their insight with me. I thank them all, notably (in alphabetical order):

Md. Abdullah-Al-Mamun, Md. Mahmud Ahmed, Mohammad Mukhlasur Rahman Akanda, Md. Firoj Mollik Ali, Md. Al Amin, Md. Nurul Amin, Md. Ahsan Ullah Bhuiyan, Bikash Kumar Das, Dr. M.S. Islam, Md. Abdul Gofran, Pinaki Sen Gupta, Md. Fazlul Haque, Md. Majbabul Haque, Md. Quamrul Haque, Md. Rofiqul Haque, Md. Delwar Hossain, Md. Faruque Hossain, Rubina Hussain, Md. Azizul Islam, Rezaul Islam, Md. Sirajul, Islam, Shaikh Fahad Bin Habib, Md. Hadisuzzaman, Rezaul Karim, Dr. A.M. Hasan Rashid Khan, Md. Nurul Amin Khandaker, Itu Khisha, Md. Golam Mostofa, Md. Fazley Rabbi, ABM Moinur Rahman, Md. Rejaun-Nabi-Raja, Md. Wasim Reza, Md. Abdul Mannan Sarker, Nur Mohammad Sarker, Prodip Kumar Sarker, Faruk Ahmed Sarker, Md. Jalal Uddin, Fakir Moslem Uddin.

Words cannot express my gratitude to Shakti's competent branch- and regional-managers, its energetic field staff and the exceptional Grameen Technology Center engineers, who taught me what works and were not afraid to voice complaints or admit mistakes. All of them, who are too many to name, have helped create this book.

I thank Alex Counts for introducing me to Bangladesh, Zainul Abedin and Mahmud Ull Haq for introducing me to the Bengali culture. I thank Dr.

Eric Martinot for sharing his research with me and I remain grateful to the late Dr. Hermann Scheer who encouraged my work on rural electrification in developing countries early on.

I am obliged to the former Grameen Shakti managers, Dr. Md. Anisuzzaman and Md. Ruhul Quddus for guiding me through the early years of Grameen Shakti's development and I thank Dipal C. Barua and his kind family for hosting me.

Foreword

Nancy Wimmer has been a great friend of Grameen. She has been closely following the developments at Grameen Shakti and other Grameen companies over the years now; and it is with pleasure that I write the foreword to this book *Green Energy for a Billion Poor*.

In the early nineties over 70% of Bangladesh was not connected to the national grid (the situation has not changed much since then). This had a tremendous impact on the economic lives of people. After sunset, when darkness fell, all activities came to an end. I thought that if it was possible to provide the people with light, then their lives could improve tremendously—people could continue with their economic activities well into the darkness, and their children could study at night. We participated in international conferences on renewable energy. We got a broader energy picture and the threat of global warming from these conferences. These inspired us to do something concrete. So in 1996 I started Grameen Shakti with a simple idea: to bring electricity to people in rural Bangladesh with solar energy. Many people argued that it could not be done, the difficulties could not be overcome; but I was determined to try nevertheless.

Today Grameen Shakti is a thriving business enterprise on a social mission. It has installed nearly 700,000 Solar Home Systems (SHS) and is on course to installing 1 million by the end of 2011. By 2015, we hope to reach a target of 5 million solar home systems installed in Bangladesh. In the beginning of Grameen Shakti, we had difficulty in selling twenty-five systems per month. Now we have come to a stage where we are selling over a thousand solar systems per day. That number will jump dramatically if the cost of the solar panel goes down sharply. Grameen Shakti has proven that the renewable energy sector is an excellent sector for social business. The seed of the social business has been developed through the experimentations of Grameen Shakti. The model has been proven; now all that needs to be done is to plant thousands of these seeds around the world.

One thing that is holding back the market for solar energy is the price of a photovoltaic panel. Today, the cost per watt ranges from US$1.70 to $2.00. I keep on hoping that the technological innovations will drastically reduce the cost of solar power generation. When it happens, it will become a very attractive source of energy in the world. Grameen Shakti has opened a door of possibilities. It has dispelled the myth that renewable energy has to remain bounded by the limits of subsidies afforded by governments or donors; that free or near free distribution of solar panels is its only fate. Grameen Shakti has drawn attention to the fact that renewable energy is an excellent area for social business both in production and in distribution. It is a good example of cause-driven business, where business can be done to achieve environmental goals, rather than make personal financial gain.

Another issue needs immediate attention. That is the issue of the storage battery used in the solar home systems. When we are selling a thousand solar systems per day, we are also selling a thousand batteries per day as an essential component of the solar systems. We don't feel comfortable with this because these batteries are not environmentally clean. We are hoping that battery technology will change to make the batteries environmentally friendly. We see some developments in that direction. One big change is coming from the auto makers, who are devoting enormous resources to developing electric cars. Electric car makers are concerned about the environment credentials of these batteries.

We are looking forward to a breakthrough in expanding the outreach of renewable energy in the rural areas of Bangladesh. We are exploring the possibility of creating a simple vehicle, which will carry these heavy electric car batteries around, powered by the batteries themselves. With this, we will get *mobile batteries* which can be driven to the spots where energy is needed at the specific time of the day or night. It can irrigate agricultural fields, or run machines in a rural factory during daytime, provide electricity at home or marketplace during night, carry the agricultural produce from the field to the marketplace, and provide mobility to the owner of the mobile battery.

To make it easy for the mobile battery owners, many battery charging stations or battery exchange stations, will spring up at strategic locations in the rural areas. The mobile battery will be driven up to these stations to exchange the exhausted battery with a fully charged battery. Battery stations themselves can become the producers of electricity for a local renewable energy mini-grid. On special days of village celebrations all the mobile batteries of the village can assemble at the celebration point to light up a whole area to enjoy a football game or a wedding ceremony. Villages will no longer be in the Dark Age.

With the synergy between photovoltaic technology and clean battery technology, it is possible to create an environment friendly life-style and economy for the vast majority of the people around the world. Financial incentives provided by the Clean Development Mechanism (CDM) can make it expand very fast.

Grameen Shakti is also popularizing biogas technology by making people aware of the benefits of generating biogas for cooking and lighting while producing organic fertilizer. Growth of biogas is still slow in Grameen Shakti. We are trying to pick up the speed from the present level of 16,000 biogas plants installed to a total of 200,000 biogas plants in 2015.

Clean cooking stoves are picking up speed as we improve our production and distribution model. In 2011, we will have a total of half a million clean cooking stoves installed. By 2015, our goal is to reach a total of 5 million stoves, reaching a target of selling five thousand cooking stoves per day.

As our young staff in the villages demonstrates every day that environmental goals can be reached in a sustainable way, we become more and more confident that people are ready to adapt their life-style consistent with the safety and sustainability of the planet. Given the opportunity, they will willingly opt for such an option. Only our technology, business models, financing mechanisms and public policies have to be aligned with it.

I congratulate Nancy Wimmer for getting interested in the activities of Grameen Shakti and studying it so deeply to bring out what makes it work. She did not stop at presenting the philosophy and the impressive results produced by Grameen Shakti, she went beyond them to discover and understand the foot soldiers-cum-creators of Grameen Shakti. That makes this book very unique. It also tells the reader how passionate the writer is about the dedication and commitment of these young people, delivering a product that will change the world.

I hope the readers will be inspired by the stories told by the author, as well as by the painstaking ways she has collected her stories, and by the passion with which she has presented these stories to the world.

Professor Muhammad Yunus
Founder, Grameen Shakti

Contents

Bangladesh and its capital Dhaka

Part One

The Days of the Pioneers

1996–2003

Installation of a solar home system by Grameen Shakti's first branch in Dhalapara

1

Bootstrapping in the Hinterland

The Grameen Way of Doing Business

Hundreds of excited people crowded the village schoolyard. Students had stacked a few benches on top of each other for a make-shift platform. As the young engineer climbed onto the shaky stage, the crowd quieted in anticipation. The engineer held a small battery-operated radio in his hand. He raised it over his head. The crowd could hear music being played from a local radio station. Then he removed the battery, showed it to the crowd, and hooked the radio to a half-watt solar panel. The music played on the radio without the battery. The amazed crowd shouted *"Jadukor!* You must be a magician."

The young engineer laughed and explained that the solar panel was not magic, but simply making use of something Bangladesh has plenty of— sunlight. "The energy comes from the sun," he told the astonished students, "something which has fascinated scientists for hundreds of years. A century ago, a young French physicist discovered the solar cell. Scientists later experimented with generating solar electricity to provide power aboard a spacecraft. During the oil crisis in the 1970s the President of the United States had solar panels installed on the roof of the White House. People use solar power to run pocket calculators in Japan. And now, after so many years have passed, solar technology is here—in your village."

What seemed like magic to the people on that village field was nothing more than the solar power generated by a tiny half-watt panel. Far more incredible would be the ripple effect this was to cause in the community in the years to come. No one listening to that solar-powered radio had anything better at home than candles and kerosene lanterns for light and batteries to power radios and televisions. More than a hundred million people in rural Bangladesh had no access to the electric grid and little chance of getting it in future. The grid expanded so slowly to remote villages that most young people would not enjoy the benefit of electricity in their lifetime.

In 1995, the Grameen Bank decided to address the problem of a lack of grid access and began exploring alternatives to grid electricity for its more than two million borrowers in rural Bangladesh. The time was right. Twenty years of Grameen Bank experience had demonstrated that the rural poor can successfully start small businesses with access to microcredit. To further support its borrowers, the bank had introduced loans for family enterprises and houses: A house offers a safe dry space to work the year round. But most of these businesses needed electricity to prosper.

The bank first asked energy experts to work together with its engineering department. They installed solar systems in Grameen borrowers' houses on an experimental basis and explored the renewable energy options available. A decentralized power supply with solar home systems seemed best suited to rural households. Except for the price.

"I thought we should go on experimenting even if the solar systems were expensive," recalls Professor Muhammad Yunus, founder of the Grameen Bank and Nobel Laureate. "The solar home system experiment excited me. Rural demand for energy was huge and solar technology available. For the first time I felt this could be done if we could find ways to make solar systems affordable as a consumer product. But I wanted to proceed in a business way."

During the following months, preparations were made to establish a new Grameen company to bring renewable energy at affordable cost to rural communities. In June 1996, Grameen Shakti, which means *village energy*, was founded as the first renewable energy service company in rural Bangladesh. As a rural business, it had to create a market for solar systems through improving the quality of village life. Solar technology was expensive; therefore its benefit to the rural population had to be substantial.

Development experts inside and outside Bangladesh were skeptical. They argued that Grameen had not yet done enough research, that income generation with solar systems might be the Grameen way of doing business, but that it was idealistic when compared to the harsh realities of the rural energy market. A market-based approach in a poor developing country? Out of the question.

"People told me the same thing back in 1976 when we began giving tiny loans to the poor," countered the founder of the Grameen Bank. "They said the poor can't pay back; you'll have to subsidize the loans. They told me the same thing again in 1984 when the bank introduced House Loans. But the critics were wrong. The poor paid back their loans. Then why should it be impossible to provide solar electricity to village people who desperately need it? We must show it can be done. Otherwise no one will believe it."

Grameen Shakti set up its first demonstration point with a 17W solar panel with two lamps at a Grameen Bank branch with no grid connection and a second one at the home of a Grameen Bank borrower nearby. Both demonstration points were located in Kalihati, where the Grameen Bank had been working since 1980 and was well known and respected in the community. Kalihati is located in the district of Tangail, just north of Dhaka, the Bangladesh capital, so Shakti managers could join their bank colleagues for solar demonstrations they hoped would attract large numbers of villagers. But this was not really difficult in Bangladesh, where anything unusual is a crowd magnet.

The first time a solar light is switched on is an event. The excitement is tangible. People are mesmerized at the sight of bright light which appears with the flick of a switch. For most villagers, it is their first encounter with electric light. Shakti managers would sometimes stay overnight in the village just to see people's reactions when the solar lamp was switched on again the following day. If there was any magic in solar power, it was the enthusiasm it sparked when the lights went on. For a moment, everyone forgot about the cost. Electric light was in the village. It was the beginning of an exciting new era.

Planting the seed

As a newly founded company, Shakti was hard pressed to find out how to run a solar business in a rural environment. As important as Grameen Bank's support was at the start, microcredit was an altogether different business than marketing a technical product. Village people understood loans, but not solar power. They were aware of their need for electricity, but thought it could only come from the grid. Alternative sources of power were exotic.

A unique program had to be developed to reach a population that was skeptical of a technology that seemed like magic since it could not be seen, like the power lines of the electric grid. Shakti thus first focused on how people could benefit from solar power and learned that children's studies at night were a top priority for mothers. Shakti probed further and heard from a sawmill owner about how dangerous it was to work after dark, from an electrician about the problems with a kerosene cooker to heat up his soldering iron, and—best of all—about how a grocery shop owner and a carpenter earned extra money on the side by using their solar lamps.

Shakti managers attended international seminars, talked with energy experts, and evaluated case studies in the hope of learning more about running a solar company. But the more they heard about conventional ways of doing solar business, the more they thought they weren't in the same business at all.

Shakti was doing something entirely different. It was learning directly from its potential customers. Its approach was bottom-up, trial and error, open to new information and experiences. An experiment with no desire to become a theory. An endeavor to create a sustainable business.

When Shakti discovered what best suited one villager's needs, it tried it on a few dozen people, then a few hundred, and then fine-tuned the process until it ran smoothly. As a pioneer in an unexplored market, Shakti focused on creating a product people enjoy—something that piques their curiosity and creates excitement in the village when talking about it. Prof. Yunus, the founder of Grameen Bank, had designed microcredit the same way and later described the process: "If your work has a positive impact on five to ten people, you have invented a seed. Now you can plant it a million times."

Grameen Shakti grew its solar business to such an extent that by 2010, it had reached more than half a million customers straight from these experiences and learned from scratch in the villages of Bangladesh. The start-up company's main assets would be the motivated staff it had yet to assemble. Its feedback would come directly from the village. And its teachers would be its creative customers.

Bootstrapping Grameen Shakti

"We will make electricity so cheap that only the rich will burn candles," predicted a young and optimistic Thomas Edison when demonstrating electric light in 1879. But Menlo Park, New Jersey, where he worked in the United States is a long way from Kalihati in Bangladesh, and not only in distance. American cities at that time were already industrialized and ready to become major markets for electricity and the telephone. More than a hundred years later, Bangladesh was still an undeveloped agrarian society. In 1995, only 9 percent of its rural households were connected to the grid.

There was no electric grid in Kalihati, and when Shakti finally did introduce solar power to the rural population, it was anything but cheap. For the 13,000 Taka (US$317) a 17W solar home system cost in 1996, villagers could have bought more than three thousand candles. Many of the rural poor earned little more than that in half a year. A Grameen Bank loan averaged US$100 to start a small business.

The prohibitive cost of a solar home system at that time was a major problem for the start-up renewable energy company, and Shakti was challenged to find unconventional solutions. But this was only one of Shakti's major challenges when launching its solar business. Shakti managers had to set up a new network of branches, staff a new company, master a new technology, and develop a new market.

Edison's observation that success is 1 percent inspiration and 99 percent perspiration thus comes closer to characterizing the Grameen Shakti experience. The company began operations with modest funding, a small office in the Grameen Bank building, and a small team: an engineer on leave from Grameen Technology Department, managers for accounts and administration, a field operations supervisor, and a newly appointed managing director with years of experience at Grameen Bank.

Shakti expanded slowly and kept organizational costs to a minimum until it better understood the market. In September 1996, it hired a young engineer to open its first branch office in Dhalapara, about 20 kilometers from Kalihati. He quickly won the trust of the locals and, with the support of Shakti's head office engineer and the Grameen Bank Dhalapara Branch, he soon was installing several solar systems a month. His first customer, Mr. Hossain, provided a room in his home to house the first branch office.

Shakti had only a handful of customers, but was already learning the essentials of its future market. Customer number twelve, for example, provided some interesting lessons. He bought a 48W solar system for 22,000 Taka, made a down payment of 11,000 Taka, and agreed to pay off the rest in six months. As it turned out, this customer took a full five years to pay off his installments. He paid because branch engineers never gave up making personal visits to his house to politely remind him. Sometimes payment amounted to only 200 Taka, but in the end the branch staff's persistence won out. Shakti understands the village mindset. This is one of the reasons why the company is still in business today.

Entering an Unexplored Market

Shakti managers knew never to underestimate the rural people and focused on how to make a new product attractive by appealing to villagers' common sense. They began by distributing leaflets showing the cost of kerosene and batteries (the two most common sources of energy at the time) and then comparing this cost to the benefits of solar-powered light. They demonstrated solar home systems at local markets, went door to door in the villages, and talked endlessly to community leaders, teachers, and business people. They learned what people needed electricity for most, about their frustrations with kerosene lanterns, and what they would be willing to pay for. The solar energy market then was essentially a stream of information flowing into Shakti's future business. In time Shakti learned to interpret its meaning.

Shakti found a decentralized power supply best suited to rural households and made solar home systems the focus of its renewable energy business. Solar home system technology is sophisticated, but the installation of the solar panel, battery, and charge controller is essentially plug and play, and its basic maintenance is quickly mastered. It is also a cheaper and simpler alternative to biogas plants, which require a larger investment and up to four cows or a poultry farm. So for Shakti, it made sense to first build its business on solar-powered systems for direct electric current (DC) appliances. Power for lighting, television, radio, and fans was in high demand in village households for those who could afford it.

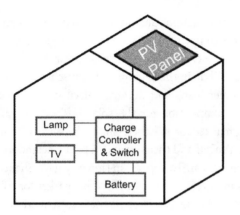

Main Components of a Solar Home System (SHS)

International companies supplied the first one hundred solar panels. Batteries were purchased from a local company. The solar suppliers provided logistics, initial training, and technical assistance, which gave Shakti time to conduct door-to-door-marketing. Shakti advertised in newspapers and took advantage of the respected Grameen name. But 90 percent of its efforts were devoted to listening, explaining, and having long discussions with villagers about how solar energy could benefit their families and their businesses and provide a clean and healthy environment.

Grappling with Cost

As it turned out, villagers cared less about the environmental benefits than about the economics and high price of the solar home system. "What you are telling us," they said, "is that your new technology is the price of six month's food for our families. Reduce the price of the solar system and we will try it." Shakti engineers responded by sitting down with each village customer to calculate how much he or she could actually afford to pay each month. This calculation factored in various expenditures, such as the cost of kerosene per month, kerosene lanterns, candles, flashlights, battery recharging, and battery transport and replacement.

It was slow going, but Shakti managed to convince a fair number of Grameen Bank women borrowers, who wanted light for their children to study at night, and some business people who wanted to work after dusk. Grameen Bank borrowers took advantage of the bank's housing loan to buy a solar home system and repaid the loan in weekly installments. Businessmen could purchase a solar home system by making a 50 percent down payment with six months' time to repay the remaining amount plus a 6 percent service charge. To encourage the cash down payment option, Shakti gave a 4 percent discount off the total cost. All customers enjoyed maintenance for three years.

This was the best Shakti could do in the beginning, because it had insufficient capital to finance customer loans and because initial progress was slow. Of course, there was no competition for the solar business in rural Bangladesh. But there was no market for it either. Shakti began marketing solar systems in the district of Tangail and then expanded to the neighboring district of Mymensingh for comparison. To expand in this way gave Shakti a chance to evaluate its progress in different districts. Was the market for solar home systems better in this particular district because there were more businesses in that area? Or because the customers were better off?

These were the things Shakti had to find out. First targeted were Grameen Bank borrowers and business people, because they could more easily manage to repay their loans and could better understand the economics of owning a solar system.

Ms. Khaleda, for example. She was a member of the Grameen Bank and in 1996 bought the first 17W solar home system with two 7W lamps. She also had taken loans from the bank earlier for her bamboo business. With electricity, she could now continue working well into the evening in her own house while her children were studying. Home lighting turned out to be one of the major reasons for women to purchase a solar home system, since they highly value their children's education and traditionally work at home. With sufficient light, women can do both—even intricate weaving after dark while their children do their homework. Khaleda's increased earnings allowed her to repay the solar home system and become its owner in one year.

Mr. Hanif, a sawmill owner, relied on a diesel engine to supply power in a remote off-grid area in Tangail. Villagers would bring their timber to the sawmill for sizing, but Hanif could not always deliver to his customers on time because it was too dangerous to work after dusk. With a 17W solar system and two 7W fluorescent lamps, he could work past nightfall and increase his income by 200 Taka per day.

Shakti discovered a similar situation with the owner of an electronics repair shop at the Dhalapara bazaar. Mr. Hossain used a kerosene cooker to heat his soldering iron, which not only was inefficient, but also was a serious health and safety hazard. Fortunately, his wife was a Grameen Bank member and took out a loan for a 34W solar system to power two 7W lamps and his

20W soldering iron. With six hours extended working time every day, his income increased by 100 Taka per day.

Since no one at Shakti really knew what to expect in the beginning, these first experiences gave its managers confidence that they could find ways to improve village livelihoods with solar electricity. But they also knew Shakti didn't have a viable business with just a few dozen well-chosen customers, when millions of villagers still read and worked by the light of an open flame.

To people in the industrialized world, this may sound like the Stone Age. But it wasn't until the eighteenth century industrial revolution and the need to extend the length of the working day that engineers and scientists seriously began to look at the technology of light. It would take another hundred years before the Edison Electric Light Company was formed in New York City in 1878. Now, another hundred years later, solar-powered lamps are extending the working day for rural businesses in Bangladesh without having to wait for the grid.

What's in a Lamp?

Village homes in Bangladesh are still lit by kerosene lanterns, mantle lamps, candles, or merely a wick in a kerosene bottle, called a *kuppi*. Flashlights often are used in bed for reading or to find the way to the outdoor latrine at night. Mantle pressure lamps are popular for weddings and festivals when people need light to celebrate outdoors.

Kerosene lamps have many drawbacks. They quickly fill a room with smoke and fumes, which subsequently are inhaled for hours. Respiratory diseases and heart problems thus abound in rural areas. They affect women and children in particular, but everyone suffers from the smoke to some degree. Kerosene lamps can explode if used improperly, and innumerable houses have burned down because broken lamps set fire to the kerosene. Although large mantle pressure lamps can illuminate a whole courtyard, they produce intense heat, must be refilled with kerosene at short intervals, and are dangerous to operate. In short, kerosene is expensive and hazardous and produces inferior light.

Solar lamps, on the other hand, are safe, clean, and bright. When an owner of a solar system turns on the fluorescent lights, people marvel at light without smoke. Villagers gather round, enjoy the excitement, drink tea, and applaud when the solar lamps are switched on. Light is there. Life is there. It is changing villagers' lives.

Light is money. People like the owners of the sawmill and the repair shop, the carpenter, and shopkeepers at the bazaar can increase their earnings by extending their working hours.

Light is safety. Women can work in the safety of well-lit homes and invite other women to join them in doing handicrafts for extra income. During times of disaster, the solar system keeps radios going, mobile phones working, and lights burning.

Light is education. Reading in a smoky, dimly-lit room is a strain on the eyes and the mind. Children and students of all ages can study longer and more easily under bright lamps. During school exams, solar lamps are in high demand among parents who want their children to do well in school.

Light is thus essential to village life. It is a commodity, a gift, a source of income.

Lamp technology matters. Shakti started with fluorescent lamps made in China. But because this type of lamp tended to blacken too quickly, Shakti decided to improve the technology on its own. It made appropriate changes and began producing the electronic ballast for the lamps in its own production unit. Its engineers experimented with light-emitting diode (LED) lamps, a new, resilient, and power-saving technology.

Today, solar lamps are a proven technology, and millions of them light up households in rural Bangladesh. Electric light is changing the lives of the village people. And light is only the beginning.

The Business of Light

During its early years, Shakti began work in the district of Tangail, expanded to Mymensingh, and then to a third district in Comilla. Through this process, Shakti managers had learned much about what their rural customers needed, which allowed them to refine their arguments for solar-powered light. However, they also had learned what Shakti lacked as a company in order to better serve its customers. Shakti could not run its business from Dhaka. City engineers were expensive to hire and reluctant to give up the comforts of urban life to work in the rural areas. Shakti needed electrical engineers willing to learn about solar technology and take it to people in remote off-grid villages

My Way into the Hinterland

In February 1997, Shakti hired a young electrical engineer, Mr. Faroque, and sent him to explore Dhobaura, one of the least developed counties in the Mymensingh district. Only an estimated 2,000 of its 160,000 inhabitants were likely to be able to afford a solar home system. Here Mr. Faroque was to open the first Grameen Shakti branch office.

"I had never heard of Dhobaura in my life. I was an engineer just out of school looking for a job when my brother-in-law at the Grameen Bank told me Grameen was looking for engineers to start up its new sister company, Grameen Shakti. I liked the idea of learning a new technology while working with a young company. So when I heard I would be the first engineer to bring solar electricity to the people in Dhobaura, I accepted the challenge. 'But where will I stay', I asked. 'At the Grameen Bank Baghber Branch in Dhobaura. Take a blanket'.

"Soon afterwards I met my new boss, a physicist, who was supervising the Mymensingh district and assumed he would take me to Dhobaura. Instead he took me to the bus station in Mymensingh town and put me on a bus which was going in that general direction. As it turned out, I was the only passenger, so the bus didn't go anywhere that day. I changed buses and went to Haluaghat, which people said was near Dhobaura. I was now almost in India and knew nothing about this part of Bangladesh and decided to learn more at a local restaurant. When you take food at a restaurant, local people are usually willing to help out. I ate some rice, lentils (*dhal*), and bread for 35 Taka and deliberately attracted some attention when I paid with a 500 Taka note. Then I asked the owner of the restaurant how to get to Dhobaura."

Faroque learned that Dhobaura was 25 kilometers away. He could go by rickshaw, but that would take a long time because it was raining and the roads were bad. His best bet would be to take the bus to the Munshirhat Bazaar, not far from where the Grameen Bank branch was located. Unfortunately, the bus had just left.

By now it was late in the afternoon and Faroque had no time to lose. He decided to try his luck with a rickshaw to catch up with the bus at its first stop. Buses in rural areas generally wait until there are enough passengers before continuing their route. The rickshaw driver made good time over bumpy dirt roads despite the rain, and Faroque was soon on the bus to Munshirhat Bazaar. Now he wondered who would help him find the Grameen Bank branch—and how he should look and behave so that the local people would even want to help him.

"To my surprise, the bus passengers were curious and began asking me where I wanted to go. I was wearing trousers and a shirt, a little different from the usual attire worn in rural areas, and they thought I had an office job. When I told them I was going to the Grameen Bank branch, one passenger began calling me *Sir*. His wife was a Grameen Bank member and he would be happy to take me to the Grameen branch office. It was 8 p.m. when we finally arrived at the branch. And it was closed.

"I found the house where the Grameen staff slept, but there was no room for me. They told me I could sleep in the branch office. A security guard was there and a few benches. But when I unpacked my blanket and pillow and put two benches together as a makeshift bed, I discovered they were different heights. I had also forgotten the mosquito coil and all the shops were closed. 'So this is Dhobaura,' I thought. 'I'm just glad the night with these mosquitoes will be shorter than the 15 hours I needed to get here.'"

The next morning, the branch manager introduced Faroque to his staff as an engineer in Grameen Bank's new sister company, Grameen Shakti. Everyone welcomed the idea of bringing solar electricity to Dhobaura and offered to take Faroque to the bank's customer meetings to popularize solar home systems. But when the branch manager heard the price of a 40W solar system was five times more than the bank's average loan for one year, he suggested that Faroque begin by first contacting the community council chairman and other respected village leaders in Dhobaura. They had influence and resources. Even if they decided not to buy a solar home system, they could help him find potential customers. Then he gave Faroque the names of ten people he could contact in nearby villages and wished him luck.

"I first went by rickshaw to the bazaar in Munshirhat to get a feel for the people and the environment and then set out early the next day to meet my potential customers. I had no map, so it took quite a while to find the first man's house on my list, and he wasn't home. We had no mobile phones then and rickshaws are rare in such remote areas, so I continued on foot to the Union Chairman's house. I was relieved to find him in his spacious courtyard which housed a large three story cement house, a separate building for cooking and additional houses for his immediate family. Mr. Hossain was visibly a man of means and influence and I did my best to make a good impression.

"I introduced myself as a Grameen Shakti engineer and explained how he could enjoy electricity from the sun with a solar home system. It was a bizarre situation, because I had no solar panel to demonstrate how this was possible. I couldn't have carried it anyway.

"This didn't stop me. My job was to start the first Shakti branch office in Dhobaura and I was determined to find my first customer. I did my level best to look convincing and told the Union Chairman that the solar panel 'was coming—maybe already on its way from Dhaka'. It could convert sunlight into energy—bring energy from the light of the sun—and repeated everything else I had learned a few days earlier at the head office.

"Mr. Hossain had unfortunately never heard the word solar, never seen a solar panel in his life, and had trouble believing how energy from the sun in the sky was to replace the kerosene lamp inside his house at night. Somehow, he wasn't interested."

Faroque didn't give up. Every day, he would set out on foot and by rickshaw to find new customers and still find the time to make a courtesy visit to Hossain on his way back to the branch and his two-bench bed. This was hard enough. But what worried him more was that he had already spent over half of his money for the daily rickshaw and soon would not have enough money left for food. The Grameen Bank branch manager was helpful and suggested he rent a bicycle for only 20 Taka a day. And so Faroque continued his daily journey by bike, always careful to follow the same road when looking for new customers so he wouldn't get lost. Faroque was still a newcomer to Dhobaura, but learning fast.

"It was on my ninth visit to the Union Chairman when he finally said: 'All right young man. You have come to talk to me so many times. You seem to be very serious about this solar home system. You can install it in my house, but I will not pay for it now. We will first observe it, try it out. If it really works like you say, I'll pay for it.'"

Faroque could hardly conceal his excitement. Only a few weeks ago a bank manager at the local Janata Bank had bought a 40W solar system; the highly respected freedom fighter, Mr. Rafiquel, was considering a 60W system with two 30W panels. And now the Union Chairman was suggesting potential tribal customers for him to contact even before he had installed the solar home system in his house. Faroque went to visit one of them the same day.

"Mr. Tapos Kuvi became my fifth customer and one of my best. He first invested in one 40W solar system and would later buy a second, which we celebrated with sweets over tea. I was on my way to building up a customer base. But the real breakthrough came when Professor Mutaleb, the Vice Principal of a nearby college also agreed to buy a solar home system under the same conditions: install now and pay later. But only if the solar system really works."

An Office at Last

It was two months of sleeping on benches before Faroque finally got a place at the Grameen mess, where Grameen Bank staff lived and ate together. This meant a real bed to sleep on, a cook, and regular meals, which would make his life in the village a little easier. But he still needed to find an office of his own. He got one offer for an office in an empty county courthouse. But if the region was so remote that it had no magistrate, it wouldn't have many customers either.

Faroque asked local government officials for assistance, but they were amazed to hear that Shakti wanted to bring solar electricity to the people in Dhobaura. "You can't be serious," they told him. "There is no electricity in the entire county. How does Shakti think it can supply solar electricity to 160,000 people with a few 40W solar home systems? People will be better off waiting for the grid."

It was Professor Mutaleb who suggested the perfect office space for the branch. He was not only an influential man in the village, but his house—with its newly installed solar system—served as a perfect demonstration point near the busy bazaar in Munshirhat. Many people were curious to know more about the professor's solar home system and really kept him busy explaining its use—so busy that he even offered Faroque a spare room to sleep in to help him answer their questions. The professor was therefore probably looking for some relief when he recommended an office space for Shakti in a building near his own and negotiated low rent with the landlord, the headmaster of a primary school.

By virtue of his authority, Professor Mutaleb could easily negotiate with the headmaster. The former tenants were government education supervisors who were not paying their rent, so the landlord was more than willing to get rid of them. But he also demanded high rent to make up for his losses. With the kind assistance of the professor, the headmaster lowered the rent and Shakti soon had its first branch office in the middle of the busy bazaar in Munshirhat.

"In a way this changed everything," recalled Faroque.. "I was close to my shopkeeper customers for maintenance, could chat daily with potential customers at the market and could now tell people in the surrounding villages that the Shakti office was located at Munshirhat Bazaar—near the professor's house—which has a solar panel on its roof'."

After eight months at the Grameen Bank branch, Faroque had his own office. He had learned the technology, installed seventy-five solar home systems, and established a good reputation in the villages. The high cost of the system was still a problem even though Shakti had extended the repayment period to one year. But Faroque now had a corps of village leaders to demonstrate the advantages of solar power: a college professor, a freedom fighter in Bangladesh's Liberation War, school teachers, a headmaster, and a chairman of the local community council. They enjoyed the prestige of being the first owners of a new technology that generated electricity. Faroque encouraged them to explain it to their neighbors and even invite friends and relatives to tea for solar demonstrations: "This provided me with a kind of solar demonstration network and business steadily improved."

There was little time to lean back and enjoy this success, however. Faroque had established the first Grameen Shakti office in Mymensingh District, but he was also its only staff. He had to find customers, train them, listen to their problems, collect their installments, and keep their lights burning. To keep customer records, he bought a receipt book at the local market and created a ledger to record names and monthly installments. As sales increased, he had to make frequent trips to the Grameen Bank branch to deposit customer installments in the Shakti account.

That meant 16 kilometers round trip by bike over mud paths in all kinds of weather, returning to Dhobaura before nightfall. It also took too much time for the solar systems to be delivered after he had sold them, because everything still came from Dhaka, more than 200 kilometers away. But most of all he needed help installing the systems to keep up with growing customer demand. He trained a local assistant, who left after only a few weeks and then had to train another. This all took time and energy.

"What I need is an electrical engineer," explained Faroque to the head office managers in Dhaka. They responded by sending him two newly hired engineers for training, Mr. Pinaki and Mr. Mukhlasur. Both arrived in February 1998, one year after Faroque had arrived in Dhobaura.

Small Team Creates Big Results

From the very beginning, Grameen Shakti hired young engineers. They were fresh, without bias, and willing to learn. One such young engineer, Mr. Mukhlasur, had been earning his living as a private tutor for mathematics when he interviewed with Grameen Shakti in January 1998. Shakti managers asked him the same questions asked of every engineer: why he wanted to work for a renewable energy company, and whether he would be willing to work in remote, rural areas far away from his home.

"I will work anywhere you send me—in and even outside of Bangladesh. More important to me is that I can learn a new technology and work as an engineer," he responded. Mukhlasur was exactly the kind of engineer Shakti needed to pioneer its first expansion phase. After a few days in the head office, he was sent to join Faroque for training in Dhobaura.

Better than any classroom, field training teaches engineers to be proactive. This is a necessity in rural Bangladesh, where engineers simply cannot survive if they don't take initiative and learn how to capture the imagination of village people for a new technology.

At Shakti, experienced field managers like Faroque train new engineers who then go on to establish their own branch offices and train their own staff. By progressing in this way, Shakti trained more than thirty engineers by the end of 1998. A decade later, engineers would number more than a thousand, with branch offices in every district in Bangladesh.

The Nature of Rural Business

Unlike other businesses, rural business functions according to its own rules. For anyone who grew up in a European or American city, attended business school, or worked for a corporation, rural business may appear to be strange and little understood, much like the early solar market in rural Bangladesh, a virgin market, which had not yet taken shape. There was no manual, no textbook to guide Shakti and its engineers.

In order to understand the Shakti story and how the company shaped its business, it is important to understand rural environments. The following experiences paint a somewhat pointillist picture that, when viewed as a whole, illustrate Shakti's entrepreneurial environment during its start-up days in the late 1990s, when just a handful of young engineers pioneered solar power in rural Bangladesh.

32

Polite Persistence

Faroque had been working alone in the district of Mymensingh for a year when Mukhlasur and Pinaki arrived for training. The two trainees had studied at the same engineering institute and were, from the beginning, a highly motivated team eager to begin work. The problem was that it was February, the month when farmers invest their sparse resources into cultivating rice. IRRI rice, named after the International Rice Research Institute that created it, is high-yield rice which needs a lot of irrigation and fertilizer and has top priority for the rural population at that time of the year. An expensive solar home system was at that time considered to be a luxury item that couldn't produce food.

As branch manager, Faroque was frustrated. He finally had two new engineers working at his branch, but couldn't find customers willing to invest in solar systems. He knew Mukhlasur would only be with him for twenty days. How should he train him for his job? Faroque decided to send his trainees to visit a newly elected community council chairman with a good reputation in the village. He told them to be persistent—but above all polite—and wished them good luck.

"When Pinaki and I arrived at the chairman's house, he first refused to come out and meet us," recalls Mukhlasur. "We were wearing trousers and shirts, and he thought we were government officials. Eventually, we were able to persuade him to come outside, introduced ourselves as Grameen Shakti engineers and told him all about the wonders of solar electricity: how it saved money on kerosene, could power his TV and lamps, and even raise his status in the community. But the chairman didn't understand why he should pay the price of a few months food for something that sounded so exotic.

"Pinaki and I persevered. We gave him more examples of a solar home system's uses. We stressed its reliability, guaranteed service by qualified engineers and a 20-year warranty for the solar panel.

"The community chairman listened to our arguments, went back inside the house to talk to his wife, and then came back to hear more. This went on for three hours and Pinaki and I were wondering if we should return to the office and come back the next day, when the council chairman suddenly decided to invest in a solar home system after all. 'I will agree to pay 2,000 Taka down payment now, but

I won't pay the rest of the amount until you install the solar system in my house.' Done, Pinaki and I almost shouted.

"When the solar system finally arrived from the head office, we transported it by rickshaw down bumpy mud paths to the chairman's house. In the meantime dozens of villagers had gathered to see what was going on and watched for hours as Faroque skillfully guided us through the installation process. There were a few delays, however. As owner of the solar system, the chairman thought he should decide where we install the panel, so we had to take time to explain the technology before finishing our work. But when at last the bright solar-powered light was switched on and I saw the people's surprised and happy faces, I thought there is no other place I would rather be at this moment than here in this village."

These first experiences meant a lot to young engineers in their early twenties on their own in the hinterland. They were succeeding in a job, which everyone at the head office had said would really be tough. They could see that what they were doing was important to the rural people. And they got a real boost from competing with each other. Faroque divided the area to be covered into three parts so each engineer could trace his progress. Every evening they would talk about their day's experiences. Mukhlasur and Pinaki, for example, traveled at first by rickshaw. But a rickshaw only works where there is a road. When going deep into rural areas, they had to go by bike. It was slow going, but when they finally did reach their destinations, they were continually asked "Can you show us a solar panel?"

Faroque bought a radio and asked the head office to send a small 6.5W panel. This they could manage to carry on a bike. The engineers took turns showing the solar-powered radio to their potential customers, which was an immediate success in the villages—interrupted briefly when Mukhlasur hit a bump at top speed on his bike and fell into a rice field. He handed Faroque his broken radio and said how relieved and glad he was the panel was still intact.

Training in the hinterland was not without its humorous moments. Once when Pinaki was afraid to climb up onto a customer's tin roof to install the solar panel, Faroque insisted he do so: "Pinaki, how will you ever become a branch manager, if you can't install a panel on a roof?" Pinaki finally agreed, and Mukhlasur and Faroque tried to boost him up onto the roof, while the customer, a respected college principal, watched the whole scene with apprehension. Pinaki at that time weighed a healthy 80 kilo; Faroque about 60 kilo and Mukhlasur 50 kilo. The two lightweights managed to lift Pinaki until he was actually standing on the tin roof, which then promptly dented under his weight. The college principal seeing his suspicions confirmed, shouted for Pinaki to come down immediately, and that was the end of Pinaki's trials for the time being. Pinaki would later say as branch manager that he slimmed down to save his life.

The young engineers were a good team. Mukhlasur helped Faroque with his branch office records. He also did a survey in nearby communities to decide where the second Shakti branch office in Mymensingh district should be established. Faroque had customers in villages outside Dhobaura county, but could no longer manage the long trips to keep up maintenance and installment collections. Particularly promising was Phulpur county, about 25 kilometers from the branch in Dhobaura. But visiting only a few customers there could take Faroque a full day by bike in the rainy season—time he needed in Dhobaura.

At the end of February 1998, it was time for Mukhlasur to move on. During the twenty days he had spent at the branch, he and his colleagues had installed twenty-one solar systems during the IRRI rice month of February, more than double the number of systems Faroque had installed in the previous month. Together they had learned a lot. Mukhlasur left his colleagues to become the first branch manager of the Grameen Shakti office he was to set up in Phulpur. Pinaki at first stayed on in Dhobaura. He would later start the third branch office in Haluaghat, where Faroque only one year earlier had begun his adventurous journey to the Grameen Bank branch. Ten years later, all three engineers would each be managing entire divisions with more than thirty thousand customers apiece.

Becoming a Part of Phulpur

In Phulpur, Mukhlasur talked to people at the local market about potential customers. He visited schools and local political leaders, went door to door in the villages, and heard about Mr. Harshed, a most particular man. Mr. Harshed was a person with *ruchishil*—someone who was fastidious, had good taste, and was excessively concerned with cleanliness. Someone who keeps everything in tiptop condition sounded interesting to Mukhlasur, and he inquired further. The locals told him that Harshed was a man with influence in the community and a good candidate for a solar home system. He was not only a prosperous businessman, but also had prosperous relatives who might be interested in solar electricity.

"During my first meeting with Mr. Harshed, I chose my words carefully," remembers Mukhlasur. "I emphasized the benefits of clean energy. How cool, white, solar light could eliminate smoky kerosene lamps altogether and create a clean and healthy living space for his family. As a businessman, he had the added advantage of saving money on kerosene, generating more profit by having reliable electricity after dark, and enjoying social status as the owner of a new, clean technology."

Clean energy appealed to Harshed, and he bought not one, but two solar systems: one for his home and one for his business. What's more, two of his customers and one of his relatives followed suit with the purchase of three more solar systems.

Mukhlasur's efforts to understand the village people were rewarded in many ways: "I had only just arrived in Phulpur and wouldn't have an office for another two months, but I was already in business. I felt a deep sense of satisfaction when village people trusted me and was becoming a part of village life in Phulpur."

The Solar Malik

Mukhlasur always carried a radio and a small solar panel with him when going to the villages, but needed a 50W solar system when visiting local markets. Markets are popular gathering places in rural areas and ideal for demonstrations. Phulpur county has almost three times the number of people of Dhobaura, and the markets are large centers of village activity he couldn't afford to miss. The *haat* is the weekly market where people come from the surrounding areas on a fixed day to sell their products. The bazaar has permanent stalls and shops and is open every day. Mukhlasur was a regular visitor to both.

"I rented a flat rickshaw van and loaded it up with a 50W solar panel, three to four lamps, a fan, a rented black and white TV, and Grameen Shakti leaflets, leaving just enough room for myself, and set off for the market. I first passed out the leaflets with the solar home system price list and product warranties. Then I explained how sunlight is converted into electricity and demonstrated how the solar panel produces electricity for lighting, TV, and radio."

People listened with a mixture of amazement and doubt in the beginning, but Mukhlasur persisted and soon became a familiar figure at the marketplace.

"People saw me at the market so often, that I was better known for demonstrating solar systems than as a Shakti branch manager. The villagers called me the *solar malik*, the man who owns solar. When they saw me coming to the market with the solar panel on my rickshaw van, it created excitement. Children ran alongside the rickshaw, villagers would greet me along the way and call out: 'Look! The solar malik is coming.'"

The fact that the *solar malik* had won villagers' affection and popularity did not mean they were ready to buy a solar system, however. Mukhlasur had yet to convince people of the advantages of a solar system over a diesel generator. True, villagers were unhappy with generators because they were always breaking down and their parts so scarce that they were difficult to repair. But people were not convinced a solar system powered by energy from the sun could replace a diesel generator, even if it was undependable.

One night when Mukhlasur was to show a video on solar systems at a busy bazaar, he experienced the problems of a diesel generator firsthand:

"More than four hundred people had gathered to watch as I set up the projector and connected it to a diesel generator at one of the shops. But the generator just wouldn't start. I worked in a fever to fix it, but finally had to tell everyone that it would be better to postpone the video show.

"'No,' they said. 'We will not leave until we see the video! What is this company Grameen Shakti if it doesn't keep its promises?' Now I had another problem. People were starting to get angry. I was certain to lose customers and my good reputation if I didn't show them the video. News of letting people down would spread within minutes at the bazaar.

"My back was against the wall. I had to somehow get this fossil to work. Certainly no one was calling me a magician now. My training as an engineer finally did the job, but it seemed more like a miracle when the engine finally started with an ear-splitting roar and didn't break down during the video."

What Mukhlasur couldn't know beforehand was that in the end, the generator's malfunction would actually help him win new customers. He told the people that unlike the diesel generator, a solar home system has no moving parts. That it is reliable, quiet, and clean. Actually, he had been saying this from the beginning, but now people had seen the video on solar electricity after watching him struggle to repair the unpredictable generator. "Suddenly they were all agreeing with me—even explaining to me why solar power is better than diesel. Seeing is believing."

Phulpur means *flower* in Bangla, and the solar landscape was slowly bursting into bloom in Phulpur county. By 2000, Mukhlasur had 181 customers in fifty villages. Faroque, who had pioneered the first branch in Dhobaura, had 253 customers. Pinaki, who started branch operations later than the others, had already installed the first 100 solar systems in Haluaghat. Originally handled by the Dhobaura office, all three counties now had their own branch offices and were tripling the number of solar installations per month. The solar business in Mymensingh was gaining momentum, and even people outside of Bangladesh heard of Shakti's success and came to see for themselves.

In the village of Palashkanda, the Phulpur branch had installed thirty solar home systems, and the village became a popular place to visit. Each solar system powered three to four lights, so at night when around one hundred bright fluorescent lights were switched on, the entire village could be seen from a distance, glowing like an island in the darkness. After a German film team came to film Shakti's success in Palashkanda, the village became so widely known in Phulpur that the local people renamed it the *solar village*.

Doing the Right Things Right

In December 1997, Grameen Shakti had completed its orientation phase and its first full year of operation. During this time, Shakti had chosen its product, received initial funding, begun recruiting branch office engineers, and expanded to three districts in rural Bangladesh. Shakti's management now had business experience, local knowledge, and the determination to do things right. It took an entrepreneurial, market-based approach, set its sights on becoming sustainable, and built its business to last longer than the twenty-year warranty for the solar panels.

As a start-up, Shakti had much more to learn, but the organization had not encountered any obstacles that could not be overcome. Shakti's management solved problems as they emerged; serious problems were not in sight, and the company's situation was better than expected.

But early success came not by chance. Right from the start, there were things Grameen Shakti focused on and things it tried to avoid. If Shakti were to advise entrepreneurs on how to start and run a rural energy service company, it would recommend some basic rules it had learned along the way and to which the company adheres to this day. It is important to follow these rules from the very beginning of a business venture, because they set the scene for what the business will later become.

A Business, Not a Project

From the beginning, Shakti built its business to last. The company started as a business, not a project, which makes a significant difference. Projects tend to have a limited lifetime and eventually vanish. They tend to pursue short-term objectives and sometimes last only as long as their funding. .

In July 1997, Shakti applied for a loan from the International Finance Corporation (IFC) and made its case with a business plan to expand operations and achieve financial break-even in four years. The business plan met with success. Shakti received the IFC loan. But what tipped the balance and led to success was the huge effort on the part of Shakti's managers to reach financial break-even ahead of plan.

Starting Small

Starting small has advantages for an innovative company exploring new terrain: Shakti could begin operations quickly, learn from its mistakes, change direction, and steadily improve. So many things can go wrong when pioneering a rural energy company: logistics, wrong place to start a branch, expensive expertise, the wrong credit model, poor repayment. For every problem, Shakti had to invent a solution, try it out, and test it in the field.

A Trusted Brand Name

Shakti had the advantage of the trusted brand name *Grameen*, which is well known in all of Bangladesh. The company name, Grameen Shakti, is therefore both a valuable asset and the measure by which Shakti's business is judged by the rural population. For however great the advantage, the harder the fall if Shakti did not live up to the Grameen Bank reputation. An unknown entrepreneur would thus be well advised to look for a partner organization with a trusted brand name. And to take great care never to disappoint a trusting rural clientele.

A Sharp Focus and a Tight Budget

The needs of the rural population in developing countries can be overwhelming for a business start-up. This makes it hard to resist trying to solve several problems all at once. Shakti chose a different approach. Its business strategy chose a narrow focus and a clear target. It concentrated on one technology only and on bringing down its price as much as possible. To cut cost, Shakti started its own production, bargained with different suppliers, and cooperated with engineering institutes.

Although the company's long-term objective was to serve millions of villagers, it expanded village operations slowly with a minimum of staff and low overhead until it better understood the rural energy market. Shakti initially focused on reaching scale only in the solar market and would not introduce biogas technology for almost a decade.

Rural Business Takes Time

Shakti engineers are not in a hurry when setting up a branch office. Instead, they take time to understand their customers and gain the trust of the community.

Two of a branch engineer's first customers show how allowing for time to make a decision is the best way to gain trust. The first, a devout Muslim and influential religious leader, was skeptical that Shakti's financing model was in keeping with the Quran. It took the young engineer all afternoon and into the evening until Mr. Mannan understood that he was simply paying for a solar system he would later own. He had the benefit of quality service and maintenance for three years at no extra cost and an electrical engineer nearby, should he have any problems. The branch engineer later remembered: "I was learning not to rush things, and this was just the right thing to do, because Mr. Mannan later helped me explain everything to other villagers. What's more, he bought a solar home system himself and became a model customer."

Another potential customer, Mr. Shakil, had been a freedom fighter during the Bangladesh War of Liberation in 1971 and enjoyed great prestige. If he could be convinced to invest in a solar system, more villagers would follow suit. But Shakil would not be convinced. He simply didn't believe that solar electricity could power his color TV. The young engineer rented a van and a 14-inch color TV and made his way to Shakil's village to demonstrate that a 75W solar system could do the job. He went by day and by night for a total of twenty-one visits and said that it was "the most times I have ever visited a customer to this day, ten years later. But I still remember feeling that I had won a victory myself when Mr. Shakil finally agreed to invest in a 75W solar system. With a respected freedom fighter's endorsement, I could devote my energy to creating a solar village. But this too would take time."

The process of building a customer base develops at its own pace and seldom allows for shortcuts. By the end of 1997, Shakti engineers had installed a total of 228 solar systems. They would install only 373 systems in the following year. Getting to know their customers in three new districts took time. Solid slow growth during Shakti's early years was fundamental to its later success.

Dealing with the Problems Money Alone Can't Solve

When Shakti began operations in 1996, the renewable energy movement had not yet reached Bangladesh. The World Bank, the United Nations, governments, and development organizations considered renewable energy a strategic means of development. But how to go about it? Renewable energy in rural areas then was often a field of experiments and failures, feasibility studies, speculations, and dreams.

If money alone were the solution, much of rural Africa and Asia would probably be electrified using renewable energies. But money alone creates neither entrepreneurs nor trust nor innovation—which are the prerequisites for progress. In Bangladesh, for instance, the breakthrough of solar home systems hinged on a novel and fine-tuned financing scheme, which made solar technology affordable to its village clientele.

This is not to downplay the importance of funding, which is so crucial for start-ups and financing schemes. It is to highlight the need for entrepreneurial companies in a tough rural market—companies that find new ways to improve their customers' income, health, and way of life. It is to introduce the assumption that the success of rural business in the long run will depend on innovating ways to foster the economic growth of village communities.

This food vendor earns more by lighting his mobile shop and playing popular music

2

Developing the DNA of a Social Business

Taking Every Chance to Generate Income

Viewed from the perspective of a rural entrepreneurial company, there is a huge untapped market for renewable energy in un-electrified villages. According to 1995 statistics, the total population of Bangladesh was 119.7 million, 80 percent of whom lived in rural areas. Although 21 percent of the villages had grid access, the total number of dispersed rural households connected to the grid was a mere 9 percent, and only ten villages were electrified by mini-grid and diesel generators. Kerosene lanterns, candles, and flashlights served for lighting, dry cells for radio and radio cassette, and 12 V car batteries for television.

Car batteries were expensive to transport and maintain in rural areas. A battery's charge cycle was ten days, its charging cost 20 Taka, and charging took one day. The average distance traveled to the charging station was 10 kilometers. The round trip by rickshaw cost 50 Taka, during the rainy season, 100 Taka.

Solar systems could provide village households with electricity and eliminate the expense of recharging the battery. But this was an expensive solution for the rural population. If villagers were to enjoy the benefits of solar electricity, Shakti would have to find ways for its customers to generate more income as owners of a solar system. It began by taking advantage of the long tradition of small village businesses. Shopkeepers, artisans, and food vendors literally abound in rural Bangladesh. Petty trading, boat rental, tea stalls, restaurants, and bicycle repair shops provide a major source of village income. With little education and minimal skills, this is the only way to survive in the rural environment.

Branch engineers first identified businesses which could increase their profit by working longer hours with the benefit of electric light, such as grocery shops, pharmacies, barbers, tailors, carpenters, and repair shops. They sat down with each of these potential customers and calculated how much extra income they could earn per month by extending their working hours with solar-powered light, and then how many months it would take them to pay for the solar system. The engineers took care to specify the solar system to serve the individual needs of each business and discussed with every customer how many lamps and outlets were necessary. Increased income was a winning argument for the owners of small businesses, and branch engineers made sure their investment in solar systems paid off.

Word of mouth turned out to be more effective than any advertising campaign, and the good news that small businesses could improve their profits with solar power spread quickly throughout village communities—so quickly that soon locals approached Shakti with surprisingly good ideas.

A food vendor with his grocery cart provides an example. He wanted a small solar panel to power a lamp and cassette player as he drove his cart through the villages. "When people hear popular Bangla songs they all gather around my cart to enjoy the music," he told the branch engineer. "They buy tea and sweets. With bright solar light and music I can sell food until midnight."

How resourceful rural people are can surprise even branch engineers who work with them every day. They were learning that with increased profit, even a traveling food vendor could afford a small solar panel. "It was all Mr. Majid's idea," they admitted. "He came to the Shakti office and presented us with his business plan on how he could attract more customers and earn more money. All we did was calculate that he could afford a 25W solar system for 310 Taka a month and still make a profit.

Another surprise was in store for branch engineers when they learned how much profit a village tailor could earn before the Eid-ul-Fitr holiday. This is a major religious festival, characterized by alms-giving, prayer, feasting, and gifts, and it is tradition for family members to return to their villages to celebrate. The problem for a village tailor is that in the few weeks before Eid-ul-Fitr, he is literally besieged with orders for saris, shirts, trousers, and dresses, since entire families want to celebrate in holiday attire. A tailor can hire helpers, but he can't do any intricate stitching with only dim kerosene lighting after dark. Shakti engineers calculated that one tailor with two assistants and four hours extended working time per day, could earn in the six weeks before the Eid festival what he would normally earn in five months. With a profit like this, engineers told the tailor, he could repay his solar system in only two years and enjoy maintenance for three. This made sense and convinced the tailor to invest in a 36W solar home system with three lamps.

Proactive branch engineers found other ways to popularize the benefits of solar power during the Eid festival. Family members who had left their villages and moved to bigger towns were often earning a good income and enjoying the benefits of electric light. When they returned to visit their relatives and heard about solar electricity from branch engineers, they were glad for the opportunity to give their families a solar home system as an Eid festival gift. In time, they also were given as wedding presents. Bangladeshis working in Kuwait and Saudi Arabia called the Shakti head office and ordered solar systems for their families.

The ability to resourcefully improve village livelihoods became a hallmark of Shakti in its early years, and management seized every chance to translate good ideas into more income. In 1997, the Grameen Bank launched Grameen Telecom and the village phone program to generate income for its borrowers as mobile phone operators. Shakti extended the phone business to off-grid villages by offering solar-powered mobile phone chargers. By 2000, village telephone operators were earning up to 5,000 Taka a month providing phone services, a business so profitable that soon many non-Grameen borrowers followed suit. This dramatically increased the demand for solar electricity. By 2001, every solar system Shakti installed was equipped with a mobile phone charger. "We have customers who buy solar systems just to charge mobile phones," branch engineers told the head office. "Income comes first. The lamps are secondary."

Table 1. Examples of Income Generation, 1998–2000

Business of Customer	Solar System Type	System Cost (Taka)	Type of Benefit	Increased Income / Month (Taka)
Tailor	36W panel 3 lamps	18,000	Work after dark 4 hours/day (seasonal work)	580-700
Bicycle repair shop	36W panel 3 lamps	18,000	Work after dark 4 hours/day	800-900
Traveling Food Vendor	25W panel 1 lamp 1 cassette player	13,800	Work after dark 4 hours/day music to attract customers	700-900
Carpenter shop	50W panel 4 lamps	24,000	Work after dark 4 hours/day	1,000-1,300
Grocery shop at bazaar	50W panel 3 lamps 1 b/w TV	24,000	Lighted shop and TV to attract customers 4 hours / day	1,500-1,800
Telephone service shop	50W panel 4 lamps 1 phone charger	25,000	Telephone services 24 hours / day	*See explanation below*

Although village telephone operators' earnings were high in the beginning, they rapidly decreased as more competitors entered the market. Shakti estimates that in early 2000, village phone operators earned from 2,000 to 4,000 Taka net profit per month.

Still one major problem persisted: many businesses were too small to generate enough profit to afford a solar home system, even with additional working hours. Shakti began experimenting with a micro-utility model in village bazaars whereby one shopkeeper buys a solar system and then shares the electricity it produces with neighboring shops on a fee-for-service basis. This gives the owner of the solar system the advantage of added income and provides his neighbors cheap access to solar electricity. But although Shakti's management considered this a promising model to make solar power available to low-income customers, it had yet to work out a special financing and service model for micro-utility owners and to test it at different branches.

Top service is all the more important for the success of the micro-utility program, because it is designed to ensure increased income for shopkeepers in bazaars, where people gather daily to hear the latest gossip. Anything new is a hot topic of conversation, and shopkeepers would not miss the opportunity to boast about their new solar-powered lamps. But a dissatisfied customer? As a branch engineer remarked: "Bad customer service and you know what? You won't be here next year. Your customer won't buy again. And neither will his neighbor." Service is what makes the difference.

Service on back roads

Bicycle repair shop

Tailor shop

Panel, charge controller and battery on a trawler for night fishing

Grocery shop at night

Providing Not Just Service, But Full Service

To Own a Solar System

Customers can find a hundred excuses not to pay their installments. In the beginning, when customers first got their solar home systems, they were content. But not all of them were willing to properly care for the equipment. Children treated solar lamps like a new toy to be switched on and off. Whole families would gather on weekends to watch television. But if the program was exciting enough, they ignored the charge controller if it blinked its red light because the battery was low. Instead, they would simply disconnect the charge controller and then complain to branch staff the next day that the battery was empty. If the television broke, they would come to the branch office, complain about the solar system, and demand repairs, because they did not differentiate between the appliance (the television) and its power source (the solar home system). Some customers went as far as threatening to withhold the payment of their due installments.

This is some of what branch engineers were up against during the first years. Rural people thought solar electricity was like grid electricity and had big expectations. They wanted to run the fan for hours during the day and still wanted light for their children to study at night. Engineers had to patiently explain that a 50W system only provided electricity for up to four hours a day. The rainy season, with its lack of sunlight, was a further problem, because customers had to ration their use of the solar system, sometimes cutting it down to just two hours a day. They also had to be carefully taught why the battery could only supply power for three days without being recharged and how to protect it in times of flood.

Many Shakti customers, even those who were better off, had little schooling; some were illiterate. It took a serious effort on the part of the engineers to constantly provide them with personal care, training, and service. As engineers, they could usually solve their customers' technical problems and do repairs on the spot. But they also had to constantly check if their customers were taking proper care of their systems. This ranged from keeping the battery and panel clean from dust during the dry season to removing bird droppings on the panels. This is not exactly the job of an engineer. But many customers didn't understand why this was so important. Shakti engineers had to climb up on roofs and clean the panels themselves time and again, just to keep the solar systems intact.

As business increased, engineers found it difficult to keep up with train-ing and after-sales maintenance, which often required trouble shooting. It was simply too time consuming to educate customers individually. What branch staff needed was customer training in groups. This would take time for the head office to organize, so it was left up to the branch engineers to devise methods for training their customers. The first sessions often began as a combination of marketing and training, as one Shakti engineer describes:

"I now had so many customers that I no longer had enough time to spend with each of them for after-sales training, so I organized an informal solar home system demonstration and invited members of the village elite to attend. These were people like the college princi-pal, school teachers, medical doctors from the county government health station, as well as community and county government offi-cials. At that time, few of them were owners of a solar home system.

"Nevertheless, they were leaders in this community, and the vil-lagers respected their opinions. I told them Shakti was working hard to bring solar electricity to their county, but it was a technology still very new to the rural people and needed their endorsement. Then I invited the community leaders to speak at our customer training meeting. As an extra incentive, I gave each of them a distinguished ti-tle worthy of their elite status in the community: honorable chair-man, chief speaker, and, of course, the esteemed *pradhan otithi*, chief guest. If I ran out of titles, I introduced the village leader as *beshes otithi*, my special guest.

"They all came, sat in a row at the front of the meeting room, gave their speeches and then had to listen to me as I explained solar technology and how to maintain the solar home system. I answered customers' questions, and the village leaders learned how pleased the people were to have sufficient, reliable lighting at night. They also heard customers ask questions about things that they, as educated village leaders, knew very little about: the use of the charge control-ler, the state of charge of the battery, and how to care for the solar panel itself.

"This, of course, was the whole idea. The main contribution of the village leaders was not their technical knowledge, but their sta-tus in the community. I even coached them beforehand to say some-thing encouraging to my customers, who had invested so much of their money in solar systems. So when the college principal—the *pradhan otithi*—praised my customers as the first to bring solar electricity to the county, the excitement in the room was palatable. 'Certainly, you can all be very proud to be the owners of a solar home system,' he told them. And all of my other guests agreed.

"In effect they were praising solar systems they didn't own and knew little about. But this would change when my honored guests were invited to give more speeches and became solar customers themselves."

All family members are trained to take care of their solar home systems

At Home with the Solar Home System

One of the main things Shakti engineers learned during their first years of customer training programs was that the owner of a solar home system is not necessarily the user. The family members switching the lights on and off or disconnecting the charge controller to watch the end of a TV drama are not necessarily the ones who signed the Grameen Shakti contract. Shakti provides free customer training and maintenance for three years. But for this to achieve its purpose, branch staff had to educate entire families: the people at home who were the ones actually using the solar home system. Branch staff called them *beboharkari*, in Bangla, which doesn't translate to customer, but to the *user* of the solar system.

Step by step, branch staff found ways to optimize user training. They organized workshops for women and children and all other family members after installing their systems. They encouraged women to become the owners of the solar home system, because they were the ones educating their children and because they typically were at home when branch staff came to do maintenance and collect installments. Women are very good at taking care of their family investments and could easily learn how to take care of the solar system with good training.

The success of the family training programs depended on another key factor, however. It soon became apparent that it was not enough to only educate the users. Shakti also had to train its branch engineers on how to educate the users. They had to master the art of explaining: not too technical, always polite, allowing time for discussion and questions, listening to the customers, and taking their problems seriously.

Shakti trained branch staff members to be courteous and respectful of their customers as future solar home system owners who deserve maximum benefit from their investment. Branch engineers were encouraged to show lenience and courtesy by recharging the batteries and doing first repairs for free, even if it was the beboharkari at home and not the solar home system owner who was at fault.

The Challenge of Rural Service

Grameen Shakti's idea of service consists of many seemingly simple measures, but it is anything but simple in its delivery to the customer. Rural service is a challenge of design: to find the right combination of the many components that make it effective. There is no magic formula. Shakti chose the ownership model over a rental or leasing agreement (fee-for-service) because management considered it the best model to grow the rural business. And this turned out to be true. Management later made ownership of a solar home system more attractive by extending the repayment period and battery warranty. This helped reduce the problem of the high cost of the system versus the low-income level of the rural population. All this is part of rural service.

But as critical as these decisions were during the company's formative years, it was the constant personal attention branch engineers gave their customers that determined the course of the company. Of the many components which make up quality customer service, it was more the intangible assets such as showing respect, winning people's trust, paying attention to what rural people need, and walking that extra mile to serve them that made all the difference. This is better demonstrated than described, as in the case of the young engineer who pioneered Shakti operations on the island of Sandwip in the Bay of Bengal.

"It took me three whole months to sell my first solar home system to a farmer named Mr. Mustafa. I had no Grameen Bank reputation to build on, because there was no Grameen branch on the island and most people had never heard of the bank. People had heard about solar systems, but in a negative way. Not long before I arrived, an organization had promised the islanders a private power station for the low price of 20 Taka per person. They distributed application forms, collected the money, and then disappeared forever. So the promise of solar power did not come across very well to the people on the island of Sandwip. They didn't believe it.

"When I finally did get my first solar customers, I practically killed myself to gain their trust and give them good service. Logistics and solar equipment supplies were the first big challenge. It took two days for the solar panels and equipment to reach the Chittagong port from Shakti headquarters in Dhaka. Small steamers traveled only three times a week, and it was a six- to seven-hour boat ride from the Chittagong port to Sandwip, so I had to plan everything carefully. To make delivery promises and then not keep them would mean the end of Shakti's first branch on the island, before it even got started. I had to show people they could depend on me and believe what I say, even if long delivery times cost me a customer who didn't want to wait. As it turned out, people on the island appreciated my honesty. They understood that deliveries took time. They experienced this daily.

"The second challenge was the island itself. Sandwip is situated near the mouth of the great Meghna River in the Bay of Bengal. During the rainy season, the river floods the island and the current is very strong. The panels had to be mounted on iron poles, sometimes in a cement base to protect them from floods and tropical storms. My customers needed special training to cope with severe weather conditions, and I visited them as often as I could during the rainy season to help them ration the solar power and protect their systems. Sandwip is about 40 kilometers long and only 5 to 15 kilometers wide, so I could usually cover the trips to my customers on foot and by bike, but had to stay overnight in the village when storms hit the island. I got to know my customers well and admired their enduring strength and energy. They had weathered so many floods and catastrophes and still they remained strong. In time, we gained each other's respect and became friends.

"Looking back, it was tough convincing my first customer, Mr. Mustafa, to invest in a solar home system, but afterwards he surprised me by helping me find more customers. He told everyone interested in solar electricity that I was honest and could be trusted. People believed him, and I did everything never to disappoint a customer.

"When I left Sandwip three years later, I had a branch staff of seven and a total of 1,015 customers. But I also felt I had as many friends. There were, in fact, times when I had so many invitations to weddings and family celebrations that I had to politely refuse to get my work done. But the islander I was saddest to leave was Mr. Mustafa. He was like a father to me. He called me the *Son of Sandwip*."

Service Never Stops

What happens if a solar system stops functioning after the three-year maintenance warranty has expired? Or if an owner of a solar system tells his friends at the market that he bought a system from Shakti ten years back, but it is now no longer working, even though the company guaranteed it for twenty years? This warranty, of course, is restricted to the solar panel, but customers don't differentiate between the panel and the rest of the system (i.e., the battery, charge controller, and appliances) when they are displeased. Word of mouth travels like grass fire in rural areas, and the Grameen Shakti reputation is at stake.

Some owners are impervious to arguments and keep calling the branch office until branch engineers finally come to repair their systems. Staff members have reported being called even in the middle of the night. Not wanting to disappoint solar owners even after the three-year maintenance warranty has expired, branch staff serviced the solar system free of charge. Senior managers at the head office were concerned about this development and decided to solve the problem before it got out of hand.

Shakti responded by offering post-warranty maintenance to the new owners of a solar system for only 300 Taka a year. This ensured continued service for one year after the three-year maintenance agreement had expired. Shakti kept the price low to make its offer attractive, but the whole idea for the new service was to ensure the longevity of the solar system.

Shakti would therefore have to think up ways to motivate its customers to renew their post-warranty agreements on a yearly basis. It launched its newly introduced service by presenting customers with a wall clock bearing the Grameen Shakti logo upon signing the agreement. In future, management wants to reduce this service to 200 Taka a year to encourage more customers to sign a maintenance agreement. Perhaps they will receive a second gift. In any case, it's good for company and customer alike if the solar system functions for the life of the panel.

Handling a Problem Customer

Never disappoint a customer. Word of mouth is more powerful than any brochure, marketing video, or newspaper advertisement. Word of mouth and village gossip can boost Shakti sales and ensure its good reputation—or it can kill its business. This is the reality of rural business.

Customer complaints usually are handled by the local branch. If this doesn't work, the regional manager pays a visit to the customer. In severe cases, this can escalate through the ranks of the company all the way to the senior managers at the head office, who then make a trip from Dhaka to help solve the problem. The case of a particular problem customer in 2001 gives an idea of what is at stake. The branch manager recalls.

"It was a spring afternoon, and I was on my way to motivate a customer who had not paid any installments for a year. Sitting behind me on my motorcycle was Mr. Quamrul, assistant general manager from the head office, who had come all the way from Dhaka to give me support. No doubt, I would need it.

"The customer, Mr. Rahman, was one of two brothers, and both had purchased a 50W solar home system. They lived in the same *bari*, a cluster of households shared by one family, but in separate houses. There was no problem with Mr. Rahman's brother, who had paid his installments regularly. But I didn't understand why Mr. Rahman had suddenly stopped paying his. He said that he had sent a family member abroad and had financial problems, but I found this hard to believe. After many visits to motivate him, I finally had to uninstall his solar system. And then the trouble began.

"Had repayment remained a problem with only a small village household, it would have been serious enough as an item of village gossip. But Mr. Rahman was an influential member of the community and a well-known candidate for the upcoming community council election. When the branch manager removed the solar system from his house, rumors of unfair treatment of a community leader percolated through the village. No fewer than sixty solar home system customers refused to pay their installments. Shakti had a problem.

"When we arrived, Mr. Rahman and some of the other nonpaying customers were there to meet us. We greeted them politely, as is the custom in Bangladesh, and I introduced Mr. Quamrul as an engineer and assistant general manager from the head office in Dhaka. We debated and discussed the problems at length, which drew onlookers from nearby houses. So now a large crowd was listening to our arguments. We explained that Mr. Rahman could have his solar system returned at no extra cost if he paid his installments, that we understood his problems, that he had signed a contract to pay for his solar home system, and that elections were coming up. Gradually we exhausted all our arguments. We were definitely not making progress. Then I asked Mr. Rahman for permission to speak to his wife.

"She was a gracious woman, and I asked her if she thought it fitting for a political candidate and leader in the community to not pay his installments after he had signed a contract with Grameen Shakti to do so. 'The election is coming up,' I said. 'What about your good reputation? Will people trust and support you?' She said she would speak with her husband."

Now all the Shakti managers could do was wait. The courtyard had meanwhile turned into a village courtroom where dozens of villagers had congregated to discuss if their candidate for community chairman should pay

Shakti. Finally, Mr. Rahman emerged from his house with the good news. His wife had convinced him not to harm their family's good reputation. If Shakti returned his solar system, he would pay for it. Shakti engineers agreed to reinstall the solar home system *before* the election and soon afterward all sixty customers began repaying their installments. Almost as if there had been never been a problem at all.

The Making of a Branch Office Network

Shakti sends its best people to scout and pioneer a new area. Usually they are natural networkers, energetic, young, and trustworthy. They work in the same spirit of the engineers as when Shakti first began operations: an office has to be found and equipped, and logistics organized. Branch managers first work alone, train a local technician, and gradually build staff as solar installations increase. Together they run all operations at the branch, organize where to eat and sleep and how to communicate, travel, and transport the systems.

Though work at Shakti's first branch offices was far from routine, it followed specific rules. These took time to develop and represent the shared experience of the many Shakti engineers who laid the groundwork for a branch network. It would later span all sixty-four districts in Bangladesh. Mukhlasur describes how he opened his first branch in 1998.

"When I began work in Phulpur, my office consisted of a simple wooden bed, a chair, and the ledger and receipt book I had bought at the local market to keep track of my customers. I had no specific daily schedule when to work and eat. It was in fact easy to forget about food, because the daily search for customers was so unpredictable. I didn't know exactly where they were located, how far I had to travel, or the time it would take me to get there. There were no shops to buy food in isolated villages, and I sometimes had to eat *cheera*—dried, unhusked rice I had to mix with water—just to keep going (finding drinking water was usually a bigger problem than the cheera).

"Months later when I had set up the branch office, my daily routine was more structured. I got up at 6:30 in the morning, had eggs, water, and tea for breakfast at a nearby restaurant, and began my work by depositing the previous day's collected installments at the Grameen Bank branch. Then I went to the villages. I had drawn my own map of the off-grid area where my customers, market places, and potential customers were located. This was an area of about 40-kilometer radius, which I covered by bike, rickshaw, boat, or on foot.

"Everything changed for the better in 2000 when I got a motor-cycle and a mobile phone. By then I had built up a staff of four engineers and a local technician and could now communicate with them while on the road. As branch manager, I had the advantage of a motorcycle and was responsible for 120 customers. One of my customers lived 60 km from the office, which meant a 120 km round trip, but this was an exception. On average customers' houses were 20 kilometers distance from the branch office. My staff had 80 to 90 customers each and had to manage village roads on their bicycles. We ate snacks on the way and met together every evening to review our day's work before eating together at the mess."

Pioneering branch managers like Mukhlasur worked on an average of ten hours a day. They kept a register to keep track of customer complaints, which is now standard practice at all branch offices. They trained their staff and grew a customer base for solar home systems. By the time Mukhlasur was promoted to regional manager in 2003, he was experienced in solar technology, marketing, accounting, reporting, staff motivation, and customer financing. He was also a skilled motorcycle driver on village back roads: In only three and a half years, the odometer on his motorcycle displayed 73,000 kilometers. Phulpur was off to a good start. In less than a decade Phulpur county would have nine branches serving 11,000 solar customers.

Understanding Your Market and Creating a Customer Base

Even when Shakti engineers succeeded in convincing villagers of the benefits of solar power, it was always the price of the solar system, which was the biggest obstacle. At the start, Shakti had only sparse resources for customer financing, and customers therefore had to make a 50 percent down payment and pay the remaining amount quickly in six monthly installments. In 1996, the price of a 17W solar system was 13,000 Taka. Two years later, 50W solar systems providing power for three lamps and a black and white TV were in demand and cost 24,000 Taka. Shakti extended the repayment period to one year, but this was still a lot of money even for better-off members of the rural community.

Shakti engineers first learned the basics about village energy expenditures and then did some interesting calculations. In 1998, one liter of kerosene cost 16 Taka, and people bought on an average of four liters per month for lighting. Branch engineers also learned that many potential customers either rented a battery or bought one to power their TV. In most cases they bought a locally manufactured car battery, which cost from 1,800 to 2,500 Taka and lasted only a year and a half.

In 1998, Shakti had no handbook on how to convince villagers why a solar home system was a good long-term investment. The convincing was left up to its engineers. One resourceful engineer chose a busy village marketplace to present his three-year energy calculation in a way villagers could understand.

"If you invest 24,000 Taka in a 50W solar home system, you will save the 10,000 Taka you would otherwise spend on batteries, battery recharging, transport and kerosene. Why? Because the battery is included in the cost of the solar home system and you no longer need to buy kerosene. Shakti guarantees the battery for three years and the high quality solar panel for twenty years. What's more, a 50W solar home system provides sufficient electricity for your TV, lamps, and radio, in addition to a healthier, smoke-free environment for your families. With the purchase of a solar system, you are its owner. Grameen Shakti guarantees three years free maintenance to keep your solar system in tiptop condition. If you have any problems, the Shakti office is not far away, where trained electrical engineers like me will help you."

As engineers, they understood that car batteries were not designed for solar home systems and that it was better both for the systems and their customer to use longer-lasting batteries. Shakti thus introduced deep cycle batteries with a five-year warranty in 1999.

Engineers were now able to present an appealing six-year energy plan: "If you invest in a 50W solar home system for 24,000 Taka, you can save more than 20,000 Taka on batteries, battery recharging, and kerosene in only six years. Shakti offers a five-year battery guarantee, in addition to the twenty-year warranty for the solar panel and three years free solar system maintenance. So you should be thinking about the benefits you will enjoy as the owner of a solar home system. In the long run, it is cheaper than kerosene."

A few years later the price of kerosene soared and provided engineers with even better arguments for solar energy. But while this was a boost to the solar business, the high upfront cost of a solar system was still a burden for villagers. They needed help—financial help.

Helping Customers Thrive Leads to Success

Few of Shakti's rural customers could afford to pay cash for their solar systems. Although Shakti had managed to extend the repayment period from six months to one year, the monthly installments were still large for a rural clientele. To make solar systems affordable, Shakti had to create a financing model which allowed its customers a few years to repay in small installments.

Solar programs in other developing countries had tried to sidestep this problem with a fee-for-service model, whereby the customer does not own the system, but instead pays a monthly fee for the solar electricity and the use of the system. The solar system is owned by the company that installs it, and many solar companies considered this to be a simple and elegant solution. The customer could easily afford to pay a small fee each month, and the company was only responsible for installation and maintenance of the system.

Governments in particular favored this approach and subsidized the purchase and installation of solar systems worldwide. The idea was that the solar company could benefit from the subsidies and then be able to deliver solar energy to end-users at a low price. It appeared as though every participant would benefit from this approach, and early results backed up the fee-for-service model.

Shakti's management chose a more difficult market-based approach, which allowed its customers to be the owners of the solar system. As owners, they would pay for it, take care of it, and use it for maximum benefit up to twenty-five years.

To finance the solar systems, management first considered doing business with the clientele of the Grameen Bank. Borrowers could obtain a loan for the solar home system and bank staff could handle repayment and collect the installments. The burden would then be on the bank's shoulders, and not on Shakti's.

The problem was that most of the bank's clientele was too poor to afford a solar home system at that time. Grameen Bank loans averaged from 3,000 to 6,000 Taka for an entire year. A solar home system cost from 13,000 Taka to 24,000 Taka. There were exceptions, but, overall, Grameen borrowers were not Shakti's clientele, at least not in the beginning. Moreover, the bank specializes in giving credit for income generation and not for the consumption of energy, despite the increased income access to electricity could generate. There also was the problem of what the bank would do with a solar system if the customer could not pay back the loan and had to return the system.

Shakti decided to handle credit in its own way, although this wasn't easy in the beginning. As a newly founded company, it lacked resources and would have to take the risk of borrowing money in order to finance its customers' loans for solar systems. In addition, it needed capital to expand its business. The solar panels Shakti was importing from abroad had to be paid for in advance.

To take the risk of entering the credit field was therefore a major issue for Shakti, but it also understood the advantages of customer financing. While collecting the monthly installments for the solar systems, engineers also checked and maintained the systems. They listened to what problems the customer might have, advised them, and provided whatever help was needed. Branch staff also used these opportunities to talk to their customers' friends and neighbors and to relate with the villagers.

Customer financing had a further advantage, which proved vital to Shakti's business: When negotiating customer loans, branch engineers learned about customers' needs and what they could afford to pay. They found out how customers would use the solar system, but also what they would like to have in future.

Despite the advantages of being close to the market, the credit business is unpredictable in undeveloped rural areas. Clients suffer from floods, poor health and business failure. Credit schemes for villagers must be flexible. What credit burdens could Shakti's customers shoulder?

Since the company was a borrower itself, it depended on prompt repayment and estimated at first that the solar home system could be repaid within a year and a half. But Shakti soon found out it would have to double the repayment period to make solar systems affordable for most of its customers. Table 2 describes Shakti's customer financing scheme in 2001, still in effect in 2010. The monthly installments for a 50W solar system for both 24 and 36 months are shown in Table 3, while Table 4 shows the estimated savings for customers with the purchase of a solar system.

Table 2: Solar Home System Payment Scheme, 2001–2010

Option	Down Payment	Repayment Period	Service Charge Flat Rate
1	15%	36 months	6%
2	25%	24 months	4%
3	100% cash payment with 4% discount		

Table 3. Monthly Installments (Taka) for a 50W SHS, 2001–2010

Id	Calculation		Repayment Period 24 Months	Repayment Period 36 Months
A	Price of 50W SHS		24,000	24,000
B	Down payment by customer (15% of A)			3,600
C	Down payment by customer (25% of A)		6,000	
D	Balance 1 (A - C)		18,000	
E	Balance 2 (A - B)			20,400
F	Yearly service charge (6% of E)	1,224		
G	Yearly service charge (4% of D)	720		
H	Total service charge for 3 years (3 x F)			3,672
I	Total service charge for 2 years (2 x G)		1,440	
J	Amount to be repaid in 36 installments	(E+H)		24,072
K	Amount to be repaid in 24 installments	(D+I)	19,440	
L	**Amount of Monthly Installment**		**810**	**669**

Table 4. Savings (Taka) made by Customers acquiring a SHS in 2001

Type of Expenditure Saved	Savings per Month	Savings in 2 Years	Savings in 3 Years
Kerosene (for lamps) 16 Taka per liter; 4 liters per month	64	1,536	2304
12 V Battery (for TV) 1800 Taka per battery; lifetime 1,5 years	100	2,400	3,600
Battery charging 20 Taka per charge; 2 chargings per month 50 Taka per transport (10 km via rickshaw)	140	3,360	5,040
Dry cell battery (for radio-cassette)	20	480	720
Total	**324**	**7,776**	**11,664**

Shakti's customer financing coupled with what customers saved as solar home system owners made an expensive technology affordable to villagers earning modest incomes. What's more, as owners of a solar system, their savings increased with the rising prices of kerosene and batteries. Farmers and businessmen profited from increased income as well. Table 5 gives estimated income levels of Shakti's customers in 2007.

Table 5. Income of Shakti Customers (Estimate) 2007

Monthly Income Level	Amont of Income (Taka)	Percent of Customer Base
Middle income	8,000-10,000	50
Lower middle income	5,000-8,000	40
Low income	less than 5,000	10

Farmers, many of whom are shrimp farmers on the delta, make up about half of Shakti's clientele. This can be expected in a rural environment. Farmers' earnings fluctuate, but many earned 8,000 Taka or more per month in 2007. Teachers are government employed and earn from 7,000 to 15,000 Taka per month (plus benefits). In 2001, rural income levels for Shakti's customers were about half of what they were in 2007. This increase in income stems from a variety of sources characteristic of rural economies.

Typical for rural Bangladesh, villagers usually have more than one source of income. Teachers do private tutoring, own grocery shops and pharmacies at the market for evening business. They own land. There are farmers who earn additional income as part-time tailors and carpenters and who do doctoring on the side. Rural people are ingenious when it comes to earning a living, but it is difficult to assess their actual earnings. There is a minimum wage of 1,662 Taka per month for garment factory workers in urban areas, but no minimum wage for rural workers (the minimum wage in garment factories was raised to 3,000 Taka per month in 2010).

It is common practice in Bangladesh for several family members to contribute to household incomes. This is especially true for tribal families, but also includes family members working outside Bangladesh who send remittances. An estimated 40% of Shakti's customers in Sylhet division received regular payments from family members abroad in 2007. Tables 6 gives an overview of customers' professions.

Table 6. Profession of Shakti Customers (Estimate)

Profession of Customer	Percent of Customer Base
Farmer (e.g. rice, jute, fish, shrimp)	50
Fisherman	6
Small enterprise (e.g. shop at market)	10
Medium enterprise (e.g. rice mill, sawmill)	2
Institution (e.g. clinic, mosque)	3
Teacher	12
Politician (e.g. Union Chairman)	2
Other	15

Tables 5 and 6 show that about half of Shakti's customers earn 8,000 Taka a month or less. By international standards, these people classify as poor, which will be discussed in the next section. Business with the poor, at least in Shakti's case, is thus feasible if customer financing is tailored to their needs.

The last installment

Thanks to its popular credit scheme, Shakti could steadily scale up business. Branch engineers guaranteed prompt service and repair and customers repaid well—with the exception of those who missed paying their last installment.

No matter how refined the financing scheme, no matter how well it is adapted to village pocketbooks, branch staff would have to reckon with the highly refined art among villagers to find ways to pay less than is due. Artful customers missed paying the last installment and apparently thought branch staff would not go after them for such a small amount of money. Shakti responded by arranging a special ceremony to acknowledge those customers who had paid all their monthly installments.

Community officials and the school principal were invited to attend the celebration, and applauded when customers were presented with the Grameen Shakti certificate of solar home system ownership. As a token of the company's appreciation, senior managers presented the new solar owners with a large umbrella bearing the Grameen Shakti company logo. The entire celebration ended with a group photo of the new solar owners under their Shakti umbrellas for the company calendar and brochures.

The last installment may seem like an insignificant amount of money. But even if only a few customers don't pay, in no time this becomes an item of village gossip. "Oh, have you heard? You don't need to pay for the solar system in full," customers will tell their friends and neighbors. How this can get out of control was described earlier when sixty customers immediately stopped payment of their systems altogether.

Shakti's decision to celebrate its customers as new solar owners benefitted the company in three ways. More customers paid the last installment on time. It saved on travel costs for the branch. And it gave Shakti an ideal occasion to promote its post-warranty solar maintenance services—all for the cost of an umbrella for each new system owner.

Customers who have paid their last installment

PV-powered lights in a village sawmill

3

Becoming the Little Company That Could

Shakti's forays into the solar market have illustrated the peculiarities of rural business. Villagers urgently need electricity but have limited financial resources. They live in remote areas that are difficult to reach. And yet, Shakti has successfully created a solar market. In 1996, few people expected that the company would have a market at all. Who would have believed then that Shakti engineers would install 500,000 solar home systems in little more than a decade? Nobody. Apparently, this market is better than it seems. It deserves a closer look.

Bangladesh is densely populated, its population young and growing rapidly. More than 80 percent of the 160 million Bangladeshis lived in rural communities in 2010. The potential market for solar home systems and for renewable energy, therefore, appears enormous. But to judge this market properly, a look at the *Base of the (social) Pyramid* (BOP) helps. Hammond (Hammond, 2007) has analyzed Bangladesh's BOP, and Table 7 shows some facts taken from his book. Hammond divides the population that makes up Bangladesh's BOP into six income segments, from US$500 per year (BOP500) to $3,000 per year (BOP3000).

Table 7. Overview of the Low-Income Section of the Population in Bangladesh in 2005. All dollar amounts at Purchasing Power Parity (PPP).

BOP Segment	Population		
	Total (millions)	Share (% of Population)	Urban (% of Segment)
BOP3000	1.0	0.8	91.6
BOP2500	2.2	1.7	85.4
BOP2000	6.3	5.0	57.4
BOP1500	18.4	14.6	33.1
BOP1000	66.3	52.6	14.9
BOP500	31.3	24.8	6.8
BOP total	125.4	99.6	19.5

Table 7 shows that a large part of the Bangladeshi population earns a very low income (BOP500 to BOP1000). Roughly 80 million people earn up to a maximum of US$1,000 a year. In 2005, the Bangladesh Bureau of Statistics supported the statements about BOP1000.

Statistics tell only part of the story, but this table provides a general idea of the challenges Shakti faces when creating a market in rural Bangladesh, where millions of these low-income villagers earn their livelihoods in what is still an agrarian economy. There is little industry in rural areas and no minimum wage for rural workers. Between 2008 and 2010 the rural population faced a yearly inflation rate of about 8%. Although subsidized by the Bangladesh government, prices for kerosene and diesel rose sharply in 2007, and increased by 4% per year up to 2010 (46 Taka per liter). Kerosene prices from 1996 to 2010 are listed in the Appendix.

You'll Succeed As Long As Your Clients Do

The fact that most of Shakti's potential customers are poor by western standards is not necessarily a drawback. Business with poor customers is viable. Their outstanding qualities as customers have been documented in progress reports by hundreds of microfinance institutions in and out of Bangladesh as well as in the book *Banker to the Poor* by Grameen Bank Founder Muhammad Yunus (Yunus, 1999).

Poor villagers invest if they see that it is to their advantage. They have learned to be entrepreneurial and flexible in order to survive. They live in a highly competitive environment and must recognize and take every advantage. If they understand how solar electricity can improve their income and standard of living, Shakti has business.

In the beginning, Shakti did only a minor part of its business with customers earning low incomes. But it experimented with new ideas to reach low-income customers and keeps this segment of its business growing. Part Two of the book will say more about the cutting edge of rural business.

Electric light may not be widely known in rural Bangladesh, but energy is highly valued. In 2005, an estimated 24 million BOP households devoted 7.2 percent of their expenditures to energy—more than twice the amount they spend on transportation and three times more than is spent on health. Table 4 shows how solar home system owners save around 4,000 Taka a year. This means the rural population is willing to spend a substantial part of its earnings on candles, kerosene, diesel, batteries, and firewood.

And although grid electricity is subsidized and thus inexpensive, grid extension is slow. What's more, the price of kerosene and diesel has increased threefold since Shakti began operations in 1996. Shakti thus foresees a strong rural market for many kinds of renewable energies—solar, wind, biogas, and hybrid systems—and will build its energy business on what it knows to be true in rural communities: villagers invest when they understand it is to their advantage. A salient example is mobile telephony, which became available in all of Bangladesh's 80,000 villages in only six years.

Shakti can see no reason why its rural energy services should spread less widely than microcredit or communication services. Its management believes all service businesses will spread ever more rapidly in the wake of information and communication technologies (ICT), since ICT will make a myriad of new applications and services possible. Rural education and training, banking and insurance, agricultural services, and many more industries have already found millions of users elsewhere, and may grow exponentially like cell phone services (Wimmer, 2008). Moreover, it is interesting to note that Bangladesh's BOP already accounts for 89 percent of the local ICT market (mostly mobile phones). Each ICT device, each ICT service needs electricity. New health or clean water services will need electricity as well. The rural market in Bangladesh is in transition, and Shakti believes in its future.

Riding the Bumpy Road to Breaking Even

It's been said that the best thing about the future is that it comes only one day at a time. For Shakti's first four years of operations, this meant solving problems day by day with the aim of becoming a sustainable business.

As a newcomer to the energy market, Shakti was challenged to find reliable suppliers for a rural clientele and was hard-pressed to keep costs to a minimum in order to grow. To international suppliers, Shakti was a minor and remote operation somewhere in southern Asia. Its orders of only a hundred solar panels looked miniscule to a large corporation. Management had little bargaining power and had to expand Shakti's solar business before it could negotiate a good price for its product. Years later, when the company was ordering containers with 6,000 panels every month, it was in a better position to negotiate on price. But this would take almost a decade of expansion and hard work to achieve.

As a company new in the energy field, Shakti also had to acquire technical expertise. Which batteries were the best? Which would tolerate misuse, be easy to maintain and repair, and last the longest in a hot and damp climate? Which charge controllers would suit the broad spectrum of solar home system configurations and applications best? Shakti's business depended on this kind of know-how. But to acquire it was costly.

Some suppliers tried to convince Shakti's management of the advantages of wind power. Others favored energy systems for whole villages. As a young start-up, Shakti had options galore, but decided to keep it simple, to stay with one technology and master it. Of course, management was interested to see what others were doing and was open to experimentation. It conducted a few pilots with biogas technology. But its major focus was on growing the company and covering its operating costs. Providing decentralized power to off-grid villages seemed to be the very nucleus of a business that could scale up easily, and Shakti didn't change course. Biogas technology would have to wait until 2005.

Shakti had to venture into production if it was to cover its operating costs. It was a matter of economics. Its business depended on the price of the solar home systems. Production would cut cost, boost sales, and let the company grow.

For the engineers, growth meant traveling bumpy back roads to their customers in order to do adaptive research—a highly pragmatic form of field research that successfully guided Shakti's pioneering efforts. Will, for example, a solar application like fans be good business? (It is not.) Will customer finance be the same in all districts and for all customer types? (It varies.) What do customers talk about wanting most in future? (Solar powered mobile phone chargers.) By putting themselves in their customers' place, Shakti's engineers learned how the organization should adapt its products and services to what the rural customer wants—and not to what Shakti thinks the customer wants.

But there also were obstacles to Shakti's business over which it had no control. When the disastrous flood of the century submerged 70 percent of the country in 1998, Shakti's business came to a complete halt—just as it was beginning to expand to new districts. For the young engineers only a few months in the field, this meant helping customers who had lost their homes, businesses, and crops, instead of learning how to install solar home systems. But in the end, overcoming these obstacles made the engineers stronger. They were challenged to use their wits and imagination to aid their customers during disaster. Electrical engineers became social engineers, without special management training at the head office.

For head office managers, growth meant providing quality products at the best price and applying year-round logistics in flood-prone Bangladesh. It meant fine-tuning start-up funding to expand branch operations. But whether at the head office in Dhaka or in off-grid villages, Shakti never ceased to follow its compass. It guided the start-up company toward its true north: namely to grow and become sustainable.

Shakti knew its rural business was far from fail-safe. But it had motivated employees and satisfied customers. It believed its market was promising, its approach viable, and that the company would eventually be profitable. And this turned out to be true, despite the odds. By 2000, Shakti reached financial break-even a year ahead of schedule. From the year 2000 onward, Shakti achieved a modest yearly profit.

Managing Funding—Money Follows Success

Shakti had only sparse resources when launching its solar operations in 1996. Branch engineers would report they had finally convinced rural customers to invest in solar, only to lose them because they couldn't afford the high cost of the systems with a 50 percent down payment with only six months to pay the balance. Management was capable of designing a financial package to ease customer repayment, but didn't have the financial resources to back it up. For the first two years, any delayed solar system repayment meant a financial burden for the young start-up.

Start-up Funding

Shakti needed funding to grow. Without financial resources, it could not create a viable business. As a not-for-profit company, Shakti was obligated to reinvest its profits in the growth of the company. It was therefore not an option for foreign investors to buy shares in the company. Commercial banks were not an option, either, since neither would they give credit to a high-risk start-up company, nor could Shakti have afforded commercial loans. What's more, currency risks prevailed in Bangladesh, making foreign currency loans almost inaccessible. In 2000, the value of the national currency (Bangladesh Taka) dropped by 10 percent with respect to the U.S. dollar in only one month. This made even soft foreign loans a challenge to repay.

To many international donors and investors, Shakti was simply a small company doing a type of business nobody had ever done before in Bangladesh. Moreover, its business targeted undeveloped rural communities, areas most investors considered a high-risk market. Shakti couldn't prove otherwise, since it would need a few years to demonstrate the success of its market-based approach in rural Bangladesh. But to achieve this, the company needed funding to generate business.

Shakti's forays into solar business were supported by the Rockefeller Brothers Fund and the Stichting Gilles Foundation (with US$75,000 each) and by other Grameen companies. The Grameen Fund, which provides venture capital to companies making an impact on poverty alleviation, assisted Shakti with a loan of 6 million Taka. From the Grameen Trust, it received 2.5 million Taka for experimentation with wind energy. The Grameen Bank provided Shakti managers with a one-room office at low cost.

Early on, Shakti invited experts from UNESCO and other energy specialists to review its solar home system program. Their positive feedback encouraged the newly founded company to draw up a business plan and make its case for start-up funding for the first renewable energy service business in rural Bangladesh.

It did so with success. In March 1998, the International Finance Corporation (IFC) and Grameen Shakti signed a ten-year loan agreement for US$750,000 for the installation of 32,400 solar home systems, whereby Shakti would install at least 3,200 systems within two years after the first disbursement in July 1998 (the funding was granted to the IFC from the World Bank's

Global Environmental Facility [GEF]). With this loan agreement, Shakti's organizational development was secured, and it could focus on customer financing to make solar systems affordable for the rural population. Making full use of the IFC/GEF loan, Shakti designed a financial package to extend the customer repayment period for solar systems to two years. It was a major step toward growth and would help Shakti triple its solar installations from 370 in 1998 to 1,240 systems in 1999.

Growth Funding

By 2000, solar technology was gaining acceptance in rural communities, and demand was steadily increasing. Shakti started a small production unit, and adaptive research guided its engineers in designing solar system packages to meet the increased demand for 50W and 75W systems. The company's newspaper job listings received good response; many young engineers applied, and there were now enough experienced branch engineers in the villages to train them. Shakti could cover its operating costs and was ready for growth.

But company growth required ample financial resources to pay and train new staff, rent branch offices, and finance the purchase of the solar systems. Shakti had to pay cash up to three months in advance for imported solar panels, in addition to the cash needed to buy batteries and other system components on the local market. As demand for solar systems increased, management needed to finance equipment in advance to guarantee a continuous supply to the branches. The last thing Shakti wanted was to disappoint customers with delays in service and delivery. But most important for the success of its rural business was the need to further extend the solar home system repayment period from two to three years. That would make solar systems sufficiently affordable for the rural population. But extending the repayment period by an entire year would cost Shakti a lot of money—money it did not have.

Financing growth turned into a balancing act for the fledgling company, which had just managed to achieve financial break-even. It was then, that the U.S. Development Agency, USAID, expressed interest in the Grameen Shakti proposal for growth funding. Its staff visited customers to appraise Shakti's solar business and later requested a joint meeting with Shakti and the Government of Bangladesh. Shakti senior managers presented the company's past achievements and future expansion plans. Discussion and negotiation followed, and in a matter of weeks, the Government of Bangladesh agreed to process the Shakti proposal. In January 2001, Shakti received the equivalent of

US$4 million in local currency from USAID to establish a revolving fund for the installation of 13,000 solar home systems. At last, Shakti could extend its customer repayment period to three years. It was exactly what the company needed at exactly the right time.

Shakti used the revolving fund to finance solar panels and equipment and replenished it with the customers' down payments and monthly installments. This cyclic flow of money provided the resources needed for customer financing, and, as expected, extending the customer repayment period to three years proved a key measure to boost demand. Solar installations increased by 47 percent in 2002 and enabled Shakti to expand branch operations to new districts. Economies of scale were within reach.

Unexpected growth funding materialized two years later when the World Bank began investigating ways to commercialize solar systems in Bangladesh, and later approved funding for its Renewable Energy for Rural Economic Development Project (RERED). The project provided financial support and technical assistance to local organizations for the installation of a total of 50,000 solar home systems in rural areas. It was successfully coordinated by the Infrastructure Development Company Limited (IDCOL), a financial institution owned by the Government of Bangladesh.

Although many local organizations would eventually participate in this program, Shakti was the only established private renewable energy service company in rural Bangladesh at that time. When the IDCOL program went into operation in 2003, Shakti had a village branch network in fourteen districts, a reputation for good service, and more than 20,000 customers. Shakti was fully positioned to make maximum use of IDCOL funding for further expansion.

IDCOL achieved its target in September 2005, three years ahead of schedule and US$2 million below estimated project cost. Financial support for the installation of an additional 228,000 solar systems was provided by the World Bank, the DGIS of the Netherlands in cooperation with the German Agency for Technical Cooperation (GTZ), and the German Development Bank (KfW).

Reflections on Funding

Money follows success. Shakti often received financial support for its business innovations only after they had proven successful. In many cases, the company had moved ahead on its own and acquired a good track record before financial supporters became interested. They visited Shakti's branch offices, discussed the benefits of solar electricity with its customers, and assessed its business in operation. Management could demonstrate it had never lost money on its operations, built up a rural infrastructure, and ventured into a vast, untapped market. Rural electrification in developing countries was becoming a much-discussed topic and Shakti a promising enterprise for potential supporters.

Without start-up funding, however, the company's progress would have been very slow. Obviously, every start-up enterprise needs financial backing. But there are many different kinds of funding—some ways more ingenious than others.

Fortunately, Shakti had some bootstrap-money, which helped it gain time to explore a new market and apply for loans. But for years, the company could afford only low-interest loans to finance company growth. The IFC/GEF small and medium enterprise loan conveniently ran for ten years at 2.5 percent interest with a three-year grace period, which gave Shakti time to scale up operations. The loan terms had the added advantage of including a performance incentive, which motivated the start-up company to achieve financial break-even and turn a profit: For every year in which Shakti achieved a positive pretax net income (excluding income from any grants), the IFC considered the company to have performed well and reduced loan redemption (10 percent less of the principal amount).

The grace period relieved Shakti of the burden of repayment for three years, while giving the organization time to expand. Moreover, if Shakti succeeded in reaching financial break-even before the grace period terminated in 2001, it would only have to repay 50 percent of the loan. Shakti pushed to achieve break-even and succeeded in 2000—only four years after being chartered and one year before the grace period ran out. Shakti benefitted from its effort not only financially: The struggle to break-even also helped to streamline the organization, to improve customer services and to cut cost.

When Shakti achieved financial break-even in 2000, the IFC sent a chartered accountant from the United States to verify Shakti's books and accounts. He talked to customers, checked field operations, and reported his findings to the IFC. Only then did the IFC approve the first 10 percent deduction from the initial loan. Shakti fulfilled all loan conditions for five consecutive years and was therefore required to repay only 50 percent of the IFC loan, plus interest on the principal.

The chief drawback of the IFC loan was having to repay it in U.S. dollars while the value of the Taka decreased, at times as much as 10 percent with respect to the U.S. dollar in only one month. This made repaying even a low-interest loan a burden for a start-up company, despite its good performance and early success. Still, Shakti managed to fulfill its repayment obligations and completed payment of the IFC/GEF loan in 2008.

Different from the IFC loan and vital to Shakti's early growth was the revolving fund, which Shakti received from USAID. Not only did it supply the cash flow needed to complete the installation of 13,000 solar home systems. It continues to this day to stimulate business growth by financing thousands more. If managed well, a revolving fund can be continually replenished and remain a low-risk financial resource for years.

Why then is a revolving fund not more popular with donors? "Because most donors still have the same idea: we give to you and you give it away", explains Prof. Yunus. "Shakti received the revolving fund as a grant, but replenished it in a business way and got the money back again. But many donors say 'you can't do this. If we give you funding for solar systems, you have to give it away. You can't charge fees.' But if you can sell your product to people like Shakti did, you can earn. Then you have leverage and can do the same thing over and over again. This is difficult for donors to understand, because their thinking is not market-oriented. You have to demonstrate how a revolving fund can promote the growth of sustainable business."

Promoting Entrepreneurial Companies and Local Markets

Most donor funding schemes cater to the needs of start-up companies with grants and subsidies. As a rule they are designed to start high when the need for funding is the most urgent, and then decrease with time and eventually stop. The idea underlying this funding scheme makes sense for companies entering a new market. It provides them with start-up capital as well as an incentive to achieve sustainability before the funding is discontinued.

There are other aspects to subsidies that need to be discussed, however. Some funders direct their subsidies to the customers only, and not to the companies. In this case, the customer receives money from the funding institution to buy down the price of a solar home system. The assumption is that if solar systems are made cheaper, more people will buy.

In a developing country like Bangladesh, this kind of subsidy creates neither a solar market nor healthy competition, since artificial prices can distort both. Furthermore, such subsidies may attract organizations that do their job only as long as the funding lasts. But an even greater threat to the rural market is the fact that solar systems, which are intended for poor villagers and are therefore cheap, are later sold by the poor to well-off villagers because the poor people need the money. This has two major disadvantages: the poor don't benefit from the product and solar home system prices become arbitrary and can ruin the market.

The Shakti experience demonstrates that it makes better business sense to foster local markets with healthy competition by promoting entrepreneurial companies that are built to last. This is especially true of donor driven projects, which can be disastrous for any business in the long run because the company does anything and everything for as long as the funding lasts. However, it's not a sign of a well-run business to be so desperate it will accept any kind of funding.

The Meaning of Subsidies to the Customer

Donors usually survey communities and talk to villagers about their upcoming programs. So when World Bank and IDCOL staff informed locals that the bank had introduced a new program to finance solar systems in their communities, villagers had high expectations. Soon afterward, when a Shakti branch engineer was discussing the price of a solar system with a potential customer, the village carpenter became angry and wanted to know why Shakti "was taking his money." "You get your money from the World Bank for free," he said. "Why do you take mine?"

Caught completely unawares, the branch engineer tried to explain that the World Bank was not giving solar systems away for free, but supporting solar businesses to market solar systems in rural Bangladesh. But the carpenter showed awesome tenacity when it came to spending his money. This, of course, drew onlookers, and everyone soon was agreeing with the carpenter. The engineer was challenged to think fast.

"Do you give away your furniture for free?" the engineer asked the carpenter. "How do you pay your apprentices? I am offering you a solar system to improve your business with solar electricity. Shakti has a branch office in your village with engineers like me to keep your system working. Who should pay me to maintain your system? You get three years free maintenance. But you have to pay for your solar system. How else can Shakti survive as a business?"

The branch engineer convinced the carpenter and most of the crowd, but he never forgot what he had learned. Nor did his colleagues at the monthly managers' meeting in Dhaka when his story was told. On the contrary, they were learning the bedrock of rural business: Village people know more than you think they do. Take them seriously. Teach them if needed. And never displease a disgruntled customer.

Becoming an Enterprise That's Built to Last

The success of Shakti's business relies as much on managing its financial resources carefully as it does on providing quality products and customer service. So it should come as no surprise that Shakti leaves nothing to chance in financial matters. After all, a start-up company in a developing country has nothing to waste—least of all money. Shakti is serious about loan management and meticulously manages its assets such as its revolving fund. But there is more to handling financial resources than fund management. Shakti demands rigorous bookkeeping every day, in every branch office, in every village. It has designed its financial services to ensure that customers can quickly repay every Taka. And it goes out of its way to prevent idle funds.

When Shakti discovered that money transfers from the branch offices to Dhaka could take weeks, it introduced policy to make certain all money is transferred swiftly from the local banks to commercial banks in Dhaka. Branch office managers are responsible for the immediate deposit of all collected money in the Shakti account at a local bank, and this is carefully monitored at the head office. If the Shakti account is at a Grameen Bank branch, the money is automatically forwarded twice a month to Shakti's account in Dhaka. Local commercial banks are instructed to transfer all deposits from Shakti's branch account to Dhaka when they exceed 20,000 Taka.

The advantages of a revolving fund were mentioned earlier, and Shakti made sure it was managed for maximum benefit to its business. It purchased solar equipment, installed the systems, and saw to it that customers' down payments and installments replenished the fund. Shakti never lost money. It understood that if managed well, the revolving fund could finance thousands of systems, since the company does not have to pay interest and has no cost of funds.

The World Bank's RERED program provided Shakti with cash flow it could rely on to invest in company growth, but was more challenging in the management of its funding. Shakti welcomed the cash subsidy it received at the start (US$70 per SHS for the first 20,000 systems). But it had to finance the remaining system costs in part with an IDCOL loan at 6 percent interest and in part from Shakti's own resources. This could amount to about US$400 per system and involved the risk of bad debt if customers didn't pay their installments. Shakti engineers thus multiplied their efforts to achieve 100 percent repayment to avoid bad debt.

Seen in retrospect, the way Shakti managed its limited resources greatly influenced the launch and growth of its solar business. Management didn't raise margins to increase revenues, but kept the price of solar systems low to spur growth. This is one of the main reasons for Shakti's high growth rate.

And yet, Shakti can't claim that the bumpy road to breakeven was its biggest challenge. "Every day brings a new one," observed a senior manager, "because money always has to be well-managed if we aim to reach scale and still stay in business."

By 2003, Shakti had quadrupled the number of solar installations since breaking even in 2000. The start-up company was covering its operating costs, servicing its loans on time, and generating an economic surplus. Shakti was on track, on schedule, and prepared for major growth. Its pioneering days had ended.

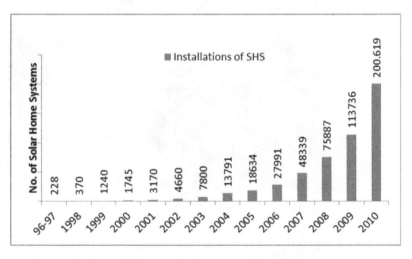

Yearly Installations of Solar Home Systems 1996–2010

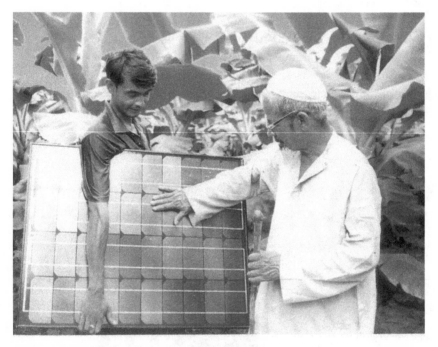

Getting in touch with solar technology

Part Two

The Art of Rural Business

2003–2010

Shakti engineers and managers in 2010

4

Planting the Seeds of Success in the Field

Within a decade after reaching break-even, Shakti had evolved into a complex organization serving half the villages in Bangladesh. Table 8 documents the company's impressive track record. A closer look at the number of branches and field offices reveals more. The backbone of Shakti's success is the branch: the ideal instrument for doing business in the village. If well managed, the branch is the closest any rural energy service company can come to a silver bullet. How the branches work, how they differ and where they can fail is described in the following. But we first take a look at where all branches begin, in the village.

Table 8. Company Characteristics as of December 2010

Feature	Amount
Branch Offices	991
Regional and Divisional Offices	145
Villages served	ca. 40,000
Solar Home Systems installed since inception	539,504

What's in a Village

In many parts of the world, *village* means houses clustered around a central square with common meeting places like a market. In Bangladesh, villages consist of scattered homesteads and small hamlets perched on slightly elevated plots of land that become islands in the rainy season, when almost half the country is flooded. Regions in the *Haor*, where the land lies lower than the plains, turn into huge lakes, forcing villagers to travel by boat seven months of the year.

Bangladesh lies in the delta of three giant rivers: the Brahmaputra, the Ganges, and the Meghna. On their journey to the Bay of Bengal the heavy flow of their waters deposits thick layers of fertile silt along the way, forming hundreds of islands as it devours others and washes them away. "The river erodes one bank and builds another. That's the play of the river," says a Bangladeshi proverb. The delta is a continually shifting landscape. Villages are scattered and houses often are widely dispersed.

This is fundamental to understanding village society in Bangladesh, because it has shaped how people organize their lives as much as it has shaped rural politics. People in Bangladesh live in an environment where the land is constantly changing, where villagers often move elsewhere and rebuild their houses. As a result, Bangladesh villages are not tightly organized communities under a single village head. Instead, they are dominated by continually shifting alliances of leaders, for whom there is no uniform designation. In Comilla district they are known as *sardars*; in Rangpur district as *dewans*. In some areas there are informal councils of elders; in the Chittagong Hill Tracts, you will find village associations or *samities*.

Anyone seeking to understand the rural population has had to find ways of dealing with this flexible pattern of power sharing adapted to life on the delta. Not that rulers have not tried. As early as the seventeenth century, *Mouzas* (small land revenue units) were created by the Moghuls who tried to facilitate their tax collections by imposing order on seemingly chaotic settlement patterns. A century later, the British—indefatigable record keepers—perfected a system to facilitate census taking and tax collections. Their division of Bangladesh into administrative units continues to this day, even though succeeding generations have moved their homesteads and the land itself has constantly shifted due to rivers. But in the minds of the rural people, *village* means more than an administrative unit.

"A village is a mental entity. It is very difficult for an outsider to define a village," explains Akbar Ali Khan in *Discovery of Bangladesh* (Khan, 2001). "Only the inhabitants of a village have a clear perception of what village is their own." To some people, *village* means living in the midst of fields, as opposed to town, where there are shops and government offices. It sometimes means the *Jamat*, the households served by a mosque. But for most people in rural Bangladesh, *village* means the immediate neighborhood bound together by the mosque, by marriage ties, and by recognition of village leaders.

The term *gram*, the vernacular expression for *village* in Sanskrit, refers to clan, to community. And although the forms of villages vary from region to region, kinship ties as well as cultural differences are the keys to understanding why villagers can live and work side by side and not attend each other's wedding feasts. They explain why major decisions are not made by a single individual, and why village leaders are invited to settle disputes.

All of the above—cultural differences, religion, village hierarchy, the ecology of the delta—figures into the formula for the making of a Shakti branch. But although there are standard procedures for managing a branch and training its staff, there is no standard template for understanding the subtleties of village society. More than anything, this explains why branch managers begin their training in the villages and not at the head office in Dhaka. The art of rural business can only be observed, learned, and practiced in the villages.

What Counts Every Day and Everywhere

To start a branch office in a part of the country where Shakti has not yet done business is often an adventure and always hard work. Branches in the districts of Tangail and Mymensingh marked the beginning of Shakti's operations. Their managers slept for months on hard wooden beds and bathed in near-by ponds. They had to scrub their offices clean to make them presentable to customers, and, on occasion, crank the outdoor pump for a week until the muddy water finally ran clear. Those pioneering days are gone. Today, branch offices are housed in sturdy brick and concrete buildings. They are furnished with wooden desks and chairs, shelves for office ledgers, and an *almirah*, a metal filing cabinet with a big lock. Gone are the days when a branch manager bought booklets at the market and designed his own customer receipt books. Accounting procedures and reports have been standardized, and it has become almost routine to install a new branch—but not entirely. Management has to standardize branch operations to be efficient and still remain flexible when expanding to new regions.

Branches in the crisis area and on isolated islands (*chars*), for example, still call for pioneers. And while floodplains dominate life in Bangladesh, covering about 80 percent of the country, not all of Bangladesh is flat. The Chittagong Hill Tracts in southeastern Bangladesh remain one of the most difficult regions for Shakti to start branch operations.

Traversing steep hills, ravines, and countryside covered with dense jungle and brush is a challenge even for healthy engineers in their early twenties. High above the delta on the eastern border to India and Myanmar (Burma), the Hill Tracts provide an altogether different terrain as well as a different tribal culture. Here, tribal people have their own dialects, traditions, farming methods, and dress, all of which is very different from the Bangladeshi farmers of the alluvial river plains. Buddhism flourishes in the Hill Tracts as most of the tribal people belong to the Chakma and Marma. There is a small Christian population, mostly descendants of Portuguese traders.

The Hill Tracts are culturally diverse, meaning different things to different people. To Bangladeshi tourists descending en masse on weekends, they offer holiday resorts on Kaptai Lake for fishing, bathing, and eating delicious tribal food prepared in bamboo pots. Devout Buddhists and monks can find solace in monasteries (*vilharas*). Foreigners and backpackers looking for adventure require a permit three days in advance of entering the region. Checkpoint police control all entries to the Hill Tracts, because political conflict has made remote regions risky. Foreigners have been kidnapped and held for ransom. Mobile phones are forbidden by the government to curb political extremism.

Business in the Hills—Solar Systems on Hilltops

Setting up new branches in the Hill Tracts requires a balancing act. Potential customers are widely dispersed and difficult to reach and Shakti is challenged to adapt branch operations to local needs when going deep into remote areas where people need electricity most. Here, branch staff has to master the problems of tribal dialects and the logistical nightmare of installing solar home systems on remote hilltops.

The ingenious ways they accomplish these tasks is demonstrated by Mr. Usha Kiram Chakma, a branch engineer in the Hill Tracts who learned from a rickshaw driver about a village so secluded, it was called *Kana Para*, the blind village. (It is common practice to ask shopkeepers, bus drivers, and rickshaw drivers where un-electrified villages are located.)

The day after learning about the blind village, Usha and the branch technician climbed the steep, rocky road for 7 kilometers until they reached Kana Para. They asked to meet with the spokesman of the *Samity*, the village association, whom they hoped could speak Bangla. Kana Para is a tribal village, and although Usha and the technician both grew up in the Hill Tracts, they had little chance of understanding the village dialect. They were met with a kind reception. Usha recalls:

"The village headman, Mr. Rum Kup Bowm, was an amiable man who not only spoke Bangla, but was open for the promise of solar electricity. We learned that 36 families lived in Kana Para, most of them weavers and a few traders. All of them used kerosene for lighting and only one family had a TV.

"Our winning argument for solar power was the rising price of kerosene, which was even higher in mountain villages like Kana Para. We explained how villagers could become the owners of a solar system in only three years, and how weavers could benefit from brighter lighting after dusk. However, Mr. Rum Kup Bowm seemed most interested in bright light for his daughter to study at night and agreed to purchase a 40W solar system with two lamps. Then he recommended to other villagers to invest in a solar home system as well, and fifteen families followed suit. Within hours we had sixteen new customers all in one village."

It took Usha and the technician a full five days to install the solar systems in Kana Para. The adventure began with a rugged and abandoned jeep left over from the British, so old that the Bangladesh government now bans these jeeps in cities. The local people call it *Chander Gari*—the moon jeep—because it looks robust enough to travel any terrain. Even on the moon.

"We piled 16 solar systems into the jeep and drove it to the bottom of the hill to Kana Para, where Mr. Rum Kup Bowm and villagers were waiting to help carry the systems up the mountain. We carried the tools. The villagers walked in pairs, carrying the batteries on bamboo poles or on their shoulders. Others carried the panels on their heads. The steep, rocky road made it impossible to return to the office each night, so we slept in the village for four nights until all 16 solar systems had been successfully installed."

During their monthly service visits to the village, branch staff came to know that the tribal people of Kana Para are Christian and that they have a small church and a primary school with grades up to five, where they teach in their own dialect. In time, branch staff built friendly relationships with the people of Kana Para. But it surprised even the branch engineers, when only six months after installing the first sixteen solar home systems, each of the remaining families in the village bought a 40W solar system. Not one of these thirty-six families missed an installment in the three years they each took to repay. What's more, all of them have since added an extra lamp. Now three solar lamps illuminate each house in the village. A second TV has been added to Kana Para and a third is on its way.

"No, they don't want TV to learn Bangla," explained Usha, the branch manager, four years after he first climbed the mountain to Kana Para. "They like watching Indian TV dramas. Only Mr. Rum Kup Bowm speaks Bangla—and of course his daughter. She just completed the tenth class in the public school and is the first in her village to receive a Secondary School Certificate. This was her father's greatest wish and his main reason for investing in solar lamps: so she could do her lessons at night. Now his daughter is moving to town to go to college. But she knows she comes from a special village: Everything but the church lights up at night in Kana Para. What was once the *blind village* now shines like a beacon in the darkness."

Sustainability Counts for Every Branch

When branch engineers have to climb mountain roads, cross lakes, and stay overnight on their way to distant customers, it can slow down installment collection for weeks at a time. A competent staff can reach as many as seventy villages like Kana Para in a month, but the need for several staff members to cover such a small area increases a branch's operating expenses.

Safeguarding the collected money until branch engineers reached a bank was an additional problem in the Hill Tracts. Shakti began operations there in 2001; the Grameen Bank opened its first village branches in the Hill Tracts in 2005. Until then, Shakti's staff had to keep the collected installment money for up to two days before depositing it with a commercial bank in one of the three county seats. This was risky and time consuming. Nevertheless, Shakti's branches in the Hill Tracts had all achieved operational sustainability in 2007.

Table 9 compares a selection of branch offices throughout Bangladesh, which vary with respect to their locations and the challenges they face.

Table 9. Branch Office Operational Characteristics in 2007

Branch Office	Division	Operating Sustaina-bility Ratio (%)	Number of Staff
Rangamati	Chittagong	107.28	7
Jamalgonj	Sylhet	103.78	5
Koat chandpur	Faridpur	109.27	2
Bagha	Rajshahi	111.64	4
Dacope	Khulna	118.50	10
Baufal	Patuakhali	103.57	4
Lalmonirhat	Rangpur	105.44	3
Kasim Bazaar	Rangpur	113.59	2

The branch office in Rangamati in the Chittagong Hill Tracts needs seven staff members to cover a small hilly area. High operating expenses for comparatively few solar home system installations is the main reason why the operating income in Rangamati is low, 7.28 percent over expenses. The branch in Lalmonirhat has similar characteristics, but for different reasons. It is a new branch and located in the crisis area in northern Bangladesh, where people are very poor. Its earnings thus amount to only 5.44 percent. Jamalgonj is a new branch located in the Hoar basin, which is flooded up to seven months a year. Farmers here are dependent on dry season *boro* rice and are hard put to meet their installments if the boro crop fails. Its earnings thus amount to only 3.78 percent.

Communities in the Khulna division paint another picture, typical of southern Bangladesh. Shrimp farming thrives in Khulna. A total of 180,000 acres of land have been brought under saline water shrimp cultivation, creating a profitable business for shrimp farmers. As owners of solar systems, many saved an average of 700 Taka per month on kerosene in 2007 and doubled their monthly income by working after nightfall. They use their solar-powered lamps for shrimp fishing at night and for washing and sorting the shrimp. The lamps also ward off shrimp poaching—almost a sport in Khulna.

Guards now keep watch in brightly lit bamboo huts chanting: "Thieves beware, I am not sleeping".

Shrimp farmers are by and large excellent solar customers, who repay their loans promptly and help promote solar electricity on the delta. One of Shakti's largest branch offices is located in Dacope in Khulna. Although it has a relatively large staff (of ten), it generates a surplus of 18.50 percent. By contrast, in Patuakhali, where most customers are low-income fishermen, the branch generates 3.57 percent in earnings.

There is, however, a downside to branch business on the delta. Shrimp farming can be very profitable, but it also runs a high risk. Some two thousand shrimp farms and hatcheries were washed into the Bay of Bengal after Cyclone Sidr struck Bangladesh in November 2007. Small shrimp farmers and fishermen, many of whom had lost everything, faced a bleak future following the catastrophe. Solar installations and repayment came to a standstill in Dacope. Instead, branch staff had to find ways to help their customers in the aftermath of the cyclone.

Branches have to adapt their business to local conditions everywhere in Bangladesh—in the river plains and the hills, to business in the aftermath of natural disasters. Their diverse levels of income reflect the diverse challenges they face. And still, these branches are well managed, moderately profitable, and, thus, sustainable.

Getting Started—A Sample Branch

By 2007, Shakti had set up more than three hundred branches and learned much about the staff, funds, equipment and controls that are needed to operate a successful network of branches. A branch manager begins his job by introducing himself to community leaders and finding an office in a busy neighborhood. Then comes the all-important task of finding a suitable young man to train as his technician. The local technician must be well acquainted with the area and connected to its population, since he must help the new branch manager introduce Shakti to potential customers. The branch manager trains the young villager to install solar systems and together they start the business. Table 10 shows the staffing of a sample branch when it began operations in 2007.

Table 10. Staff Members at Lamakaji Branch

Role	Schooling	Monthly Salary (Taka)	Age
Branch manager	Diploma engineer at polytechnic institute	8,000	27
Field supervisor	12 years of schooling	6,000	24
Supervisor trainee	(6 months training)	3,000	
Local technician	9 years of schooling	3,900	23

How well the founding branch manager performs this task can make or break the branch. It's tough on a manager in a new area if he can't find suitable candidates to train as his local technician. Some branch engineers have had to go alone for months, like on the island of Sandwip, or in the Haor regions, where natural depressions are flooded up to seven months a year.

In the example shown in Table 11, a new branch manager trained and hired a local technician after only a few weeks, which accounts for the good result in the branch's second month of operation. Later when the branch was installing nine solar systems per month and the volume of work had increased, a field supervisor was added to the team.

During his six-month training period, the field supervisor is introduced to all facets of branch operations and given incentives to do his job well: If he successfully completes his training, he will have a steady job with benefits and a starting salary of 6,000 Taka per month—double the amount he received as a trainee. Following the introduction of two new product types in 2006, branch staff training also included biogas plants and improved cooking stoves (ICS).

Table 11. Lamakaji Branch Installations in 2007

Month of operation	1	2	3	4	5	6	7	8	9	10	11
No. of SHS installed	3	9	8	7	11	13	8	9	10	11	9
No. of ICS installed								4			

A branch manager and his local technician will at first serve up to a hundred customers in the plains, or seventy in the Hill Tracts. This includes installation, maintenance, installment collection, marketing, and accounting. Shakti hires a second engineer for the branch after a hundred systems have been installed and an additional staff member when solar installations number 150. The target is then set to two hundred installations to allow time for marketing and maintenance. Additional staff can be an engineer working as a trainee to gain field experience before starting a new branch or a field supervisor as shown in the above example. Now that Shakti better understands branch operations, it is training more local people to create rural employment and to cut costs.

Because branch managers are responsible for all branch operations, they attend to only fifty customers when the branch is fully staffed, while each staff member has a hundred customers to take care of. In the Hill Tracts, the load for a branch manager is reduced to thirty, and each staff member is responsible for seventy customers.

During the first months after opening a new branch office, marketing efforts are understandably high, consuming about 70 percent of all activities. Table 12 shows an estimate of the average time spent by branch staff on its major activities.

Table 12. Activities of Branch Staff for Solar Home Systems in 2007

Activity	Percentage of Time Used
Marketing	35
System installation	20
Service (maintenance, installment collection, training)	30
Accounting	15

The Lamakaji branch office in these examples is ideally located in a bazaar. Its balcony overlooks the Lamakaji River, bustling shops, tea stalls, and restaurants. It has two office rooms on the first floor and a storage room on the third. The office is sparsely furnished with two desks and six chairs, a bookshelf, a metal file cabinet, and a fan. Each staff member buys his own mobile phone; Shakti pays for the office calls.

Like all branches, it is supplied with office toolsets consisting of pliers, screw drivers, hammer, hacksaw, cutter, drill, and multimeter for measuring voltage. To ensure prompt maintenance, the storage room holds about 110 percent of a month's turnover of products such as batteries, solar panels, lamps, and charge controllers. The branch does not have a motorcycle, so all transport and visits to customers have to be accomplished by bicycle, boat and rickshaw, or on foot.

The Lamakaji branch's monthly expenditures amount to approximately 38,000 Taka. Two thirds are spent for salaries, travel, and rent. The staff pays for its own food, a cook, and lodging, which amount to 1,500 Taka per staff member each month. Other characteristics are shown in Table 13.

Table 13. Characteristics of Lamakaji Branch in 2007

Feature	Amount
Initial investment	40,000 Taka
Monthly operating cost	38,200 Taka
Running capital	280,000 Taka
Break-even period	9 months
Break-even turnover	9 solar system installations per month
Number of employees	3

More than describing the fundamentals for the making of a new branch, the first eleven months of Lamakaji branch's development demonstrate how branches shoulder the cost of growth. By 2010, for example, an average Shakti branch had more than doubled its operating costs since 2007 and needed to install 42 solar systems per month to achieve operating sustainability.

Off to a solid start, Lamakaji branch had 1,094 customers and a staff of 11 by 2010, including an ICS specialist to promote Shakti's newly introduced improved cook stoves. Hundreds more new branches launched operations in new areas as Shakti expanded to every corner of Bangladesh. They faced all the hardships of a rural environment. But they also profited from experienced branches like the successful Mehindigonj branch, which pioneered operations on the remote island of Mehindigonj as early as 2001. It has since spawned 5 branches on an island 50 kilometers from the mainland, where few people thought solar electricity would ever light up poor fishermen's homes.

Managers and staff at Mehindigonj branch

Branches in Every Corner of the Country

In 2007, Shakti embarked upon major expansion to achieve its goal of 1 million solar installations. During the next three years, it tripled the number of field offices to more than a thousand and increased its field staff fourfold to 9,000 employees.

Table 14 reflects Shakti's rapid growth with a clear message: Shakti's business is highly diverse. It serves every corner in Bangladesh, from the poor crisis area in the north, the mango, shrimp, jute and rice farms in the plains to the tribal people in the hills and the fishermen on the vast Bengal Delta.

The table gives an overview of selected branches throughout Bangladesh to illustrate how they have grown and achieved sustainability. It doesn't explain the inner-mechanics of spawning new branches when the first branch in a given region has to be split. Customers from Lalmonirhat branch, for example, have been transferred to other branches to help them get started, while giving Lalmonirat staff opportunity to step up its biogas and improved stove programs. Kasim Bazaar transferred 100 solar customers to a near-by branch for similar reasons. Koat chandpur branch on the other hand has a staff of 10 and only 309 customers, because it focused on serving rice and jute farmers with biogas technology. 30 additional biogas plants are under construction.

Readers will remember the stories of the young engineers pioneering Shakti's first branches in the hinterland. A look at the table shows they did a good job: where only one branch was in operation in Phulpur in 1998, nine branches served around 11,000 customers in 2010. An update of the branches described earlier in Table 9 shows their progress: three of these branches had just begun operations in 2007 in two of Shakti's most challenging regions: the poor and underdeveloped crisis area and the Hoar, which is flooded most of the year. Their success in such a harsh rural environment is all the more remarkable.

What makes a branch work? What motivates a young branch manager to achieve and maintain 100% recovery of customer payments; or a young woman to become the first branch manager in one of the most endangered regions in Bangladesh?

Table 14. Characteristics of Selected branches in 2010

Branch Office	Start in Year	Operating Sustain-ability (%)	No. of Staff	No. of Cus-tomers	Comment
Dhalapara	1996	109,86	13	1978	Pioneering branch; Spawned 4 branches
Homna	1997	100,20	12	1713	Pioneering branch; Spawned 5 branches
Dhobaura	1997	116,20	11	2469	Pioneering branch; Spawned 4 branches
Phulpur	1998	100,45	15	2723	Pioneering branch; Spawned 8 branches
Patharghata	1999	101,34	13	2705	Spawned 6 branches Survived Cyclone Sidr
Kalir Bazar	2000	110,09	22	3562	Achieved 100% recovery
Mehindigonj	2001	116,69	13	2985	Spawned 5 branches
Khagrachari	2003	100,95	10	1241	Located in Hill Tracts; First woman branch manager
Kakchira	2004	102,07	15	2024	Survived Cyclone Sidr
Kurigram	2005	97,35	10	1233	Located in crisis area;
Sarankhola	2005	109,53	13	1347	Serves shrimp farmers
Mithamoin	2006	113,85	8	1207	Located in Haor Region
Lamakaji	2006	119,44	11	1094	Discussed in Chapter 4
Nabiganji	2006	112,51	11	2408	Located in Haor region
Branches also described in Table 9					
Rangamati	2002	100,60	11	2469	Serves village Kana Para
Jamalgonj	2006	107,99	9	2393	Located in Hoar region
Koat chandpur	2005	102,31	10	309	Focus on biogas customers
Bagha	2004	112,77	12	1073	Serves mango farmers
Dacope	2001	103,92	15	2751	Survived Cyclone Sidr
Baufal	2003	101,62	12	2105	Serves low-income fishermen, Survived Cyclone Sidr
Lalmonirhat	2006	98,36	8	722	Located in crisis area; Spawned 4 branches
Kasim Bazar	2007	98,83	6	723	Located in crisis area

What keeps branch staff going after its young branch manager drowned during a storm in the Hoar; or when staff members barely survive a cyclone? These are the intangibles, which elude statistics and are at the root of Shakti's success. Shakti has successfully expanded to every corner of Bangladesh and is stemming the challenges of growth. Its greatest asset is its competent and motivated managers and staff. But its biggest challenge may come from the delta itself.

House on a char

Business on a Char—the Ultimate Challenge

Strange as it may seem to begin this section with the Himalayas, there is good reason for doing so. Over centuries, the mighty Himalayan rivers created the delta we now know as Bangladesh. The delta is huge because almost all water running off the highest mountain range on earth has to pass through it. "Without the Himalayas, Bangladesh would not exist," writes Van Schendel in *A History of Bangladesh* (Van Schendel, 2010). "In a sense, Bangladesh *is* the Himalayas, flattened out."

From its origin in southwestern Tibet the Bramaputra River travels nearly two thousand kilometers before entering northern Bangladesh near Kurigram, where it is known as the Jamuna. As the river slows down and carves its path toward the Bay of Bengal it deposits new silt along the way, forming scores of small islands in its 18 kilometer-wide channel. *Chars*, as these islands are called in Bangla, are home to more than 200,000 people in Kurigram. The landless poor settle on such eroding islands exposed to storms and floods because they have no alternative. In a country with more than a thousand people per square kilometer, land is scarce and the poor are forced to live on the water's edge.

In the *crisis area*, as Kurigram is known in Bangladesh, people distinguish levels of poverty: Those who can manage to earn about 4,000 Taka per month (2006) are considered poor, but usually have at least one steady source of income and can make ends meet. Those who eke out a bare existence as day laborers or part-time farm workers are known as *monga poor*, people who suffer from seasonal hunger. In the crisis area, seasonal hunger occurs during the lean months before the winter rice harvest, when farm workers have no work and can no longer buy food. People in Bangladesh call this time of year *mora Kartic*, the months of death and disaster.

With the exception of the tobacco industry in Rangpur, industrialization in Kurigram is far below the national average, making most families dependent on income from agricultural labor. A large labor force is needed in September, when *Aman*, the rice seedlings grown during the rainy season, are ready to be transplanted into paddy fields. But once this is done, it takes two months until the crop is ready for harvest. From mid-September to mid-November, or *Aswin* and *Kartic* as these lean months are called in Bangla, there is virtually no work available when money and food from the previous harvest have run out.

In North Bengal, it comes as no surprise that natural disasters are another reason for seasonal hunger. Located just south of the foothills of the Himalayas, topography and climate make North Bengal vulnerable to floods, river erosion, drought, and cold spells, all of which occur more frequently and intensely here than in other parts of Bangladesh. A flood in August or September can have a devastating effect if it destroys a recently sown Aman rice crop. Seasonal unemployment can then last up to four months.

The combined force of natural disasters and an economy dependent on the cultivation of rice sets into motion a vicious cycle, which poor villagers can't escape: farmers lose money, farm workers their jobs, and small businesses lose their customers at precisely the moment when they need their income the most.

A Cycle of Poverty

When farming jobs become scarce, the poor have few options except to take on low-wage manual labor in rice mills and brickfields or to leave their families to go to Dhaka and other cities to work as rickshaw pullers. A few migrate to the ship-breaking yards in Chittagong, where every kind of vessel from small boat to supertanker is dismantled and cheap labor is needed for hazardous jobs.

Families suffering from hunger are forced to sell small assets, mortgage land, or take out loans from money lenders at exorbitant interest rates. Men sell their labor in advance at less than market value for their families to survive until the harvest. They're trapped in a cycle of poverty they can't escape.

Monga has existed for centuries in Kurigram. And though its causes are complex, the lack of a steady income is at the heart of the problem. This is what the young economics professor Muhammad Yunus learned from victims of the devastating famine in 1974 when he saw that food was available but the poor had no money to buy it. This experience would later give birth to the Grameen Bank and microcredit for the poor to generate income. Thirty years later, Grameen Shakti prepares to bring solar electricity and income to the chars in the Brahmaputra-Jamuna River. This may be Shakti's ultimate challenge.

Chances on the Char

In 2006, Shakti opened its first branch office on the island of Ashtamir Char in the district of Kurigram, located about 15 kilometers from the old river port of Chilmari. From the beginning, Shakti knew this would mean more than bringing solar electricity to an un-electrified char. A Grameen Bank monga-survey had revealed that 3,164 families lived on the island. Eight hundred of them barely survived on 30 to 50 Taka or one and a half meals per day. With an average of five children per family and a literacy rate of 20 percent, Ashtamir Char counted as one of the poorest communities in the crisis area. Shakti's first task was to survey the unfamiliar char and learn from the islanders what they needed.

Most char dwellers scratched out a living from agriculture and livestock or seasonal labor on the mainland. Extensive areas of grasslands on the char were used as grazing lands for cattle, but the quality of fodder was low. Some farmers turned a modest profit growing rice, jute, peanuts and wheat. But for the most part, Shakti engineers learned what was not available on the char. There were no brickfields, sawmills, or rickshaws for employment; no paved roads and no electricity.

Where to begin? Shakti was challenged to improve the standard of living on the char. But how? Its engineers had learned that a few farmers and teachers were interested in solar home systems and thought this the best way to start energy services on the island. But this was not exactly a large clientele and there were few bazaars and small businesses which could profit from solar electricity and spur the local economy. Firewood was scarce on the char, a problem Shakti's energy efficient cooking stoves could alleviate for private households. Shakti stove experts could teach young islanders to construct them for a living. But experts would first have to figure out how to make the sandy island soil firm enough to build a solid stove.

Shakti engineers therefore considered stoves fueled with biogas a better option for cooking if farmers had livestock. An added advantage for farmers was the organic fertilizer produced by the biogas plant. It could improve soil fertility and enable them to grow vegetables, which were in short supply on the char. Islanders had to travel an hour and a half by service boats to the mainland for fresh produce. Homegrown vegetables would be cheaper and certainly more nutritious than the free biscuits that food charities provided children in Ashtamir Char's schools.

Ashtamir Char wasn't a treasure trove of new business opportunities, but a few advantages were already working in Shakti's favor. A Grameen Bank branch provided microcredit and business support to poor women. School teachers indicated they would help popularize renewables on the char and probably become Shakti's first customers. And there was no competition for solar services on the island. At least not anymore.

Solar providers had worked for a short time in Ashtamir Char a few years back, but their staff lived on the mainland which had major disadvantages for their customers. The three-hour round trip from the Chilmari port to the char made maintenance and repair slow even when weather conditions were favorable. During the rainy season, service often was discontinued altogether, and customers refused to pay for solar systems that didn't work.

Shakti's branch engineers would work and live on the island. This solved the problem of prompt service. But how long could management realistically expect them to stay on the char? Shakti would find this out by setting up its first branch office.

School Teachers and Peanut Farmers

The branch got off to a good start. Its new manager quickly found a young villager to train as his technician, and together they installed six solar systems in the first two months. Teachers and peanut farmers were Shakti's first customers. Teachers earn from 7,000 to 15,000 Taka per month and could afford a 50W solar home system. Moderately well off peanut farmers with land, livestock, and an income of about 9,000 Taka per month also invested. They bought 50W solar systems with four to six lamps primarily for their children to study after dark.

This is not surprising. Most char dwellers have little schooling, but understand that a good education can prepare young people for a better life beyond the char. They have to live with the fact that most chars exist for less than a generation, sometimes little more than a decade before being washed away. Everything seems to take on a sense of urgency on the char.

It didn't take long until most of the school teachers were the owners of solar systems. This was good for solar demonstrations, but not exactly a booming market. First of all, there are only twelve high school teachers on Ashtamir Char. Primary school teachers were not an option, since, with the exception of the headmaster, they lived on the mainland in Chilmari town. However, teachers are respected on the char and proved to be excellent organizers.

The primary and high schools are part of a large community center, where the houses and main buildings circle a large field. Shakti's branch office is located there, as well as the Grameen Bank and community administrative offices. This made the town square an ideal place for solar system demonstrations. And indeed, everyone came to watch—up to a thousand students, curious villagers, and local officials. There was excitement in the air when the solar lamps were switched on—just like in the early days of 1996. For the first time, electric light was on the island. Ashtamir Char's future seemed brighter.

Learning for a Lifetime

The new branch had made a good start on the char, and Shakti made sure its staff got plenty of support. The regional manager and biogas and stove experts came to visit, and branch colleagues in Chilmari town offered support with training and logistics. But the branch's success was for the most part a result of what only a talented young village technician can provide: local knowledge. Mr. Jamal was eighteen years old when he started training with the branch engineer and describes how his work began in 2006.

> "It was September towards the end of the rainy season and not exactly the best time of the year to be marketing solar systems. So I was actually surprised when we managed to convince four customers in one month to purchase a solar home system. I thought the branch manager had chosen to train me because I lived next door to his office and didn't have a job—when actually he had chosen me because he needed my help to gain the trust of the islanders. This gave me confidence and I worked hard. By the time the branch manager left at the end of 2007, I had helped to install a total of 79 solar systems and train two more local technicians."

What this story doesn't tell us is why Jamal contributes far more to the success of the branch than just knowing the villagers. With an area of 225 square kilometers, Ashtamir Char is not overly large. The difficulty lies in serving customers during 40° C heat in summer, when one can neither walk nor bike on the hot sand, and in working in torrential rains on unpaved roads in the monsoon season. The new branch manager explains:

> "It takes four men and two bicycles to carry the battery and panel. There are no rickshaws here. If we have to deliver to customers living on other chars, we must transport the solar systems on bikes to the shore and then hope to find a boat to take us to our destination. Boats are especially hard to find in the rainy season when the river is high and chars are flooded. The only advantage is that the boat can dock closer to the chars during floods and we don't have so far to walk to the customers.

> "I sometimes wonder how I can continue this job on the char. The food is bland, vegetables are not fresh. The intense heat and rain

are seasonal shocks. I would like to marry, but would my future wife want to live on the char? And still, I admit it's fascinating to see how solar electricity is changing the lives of the islanders.

"People on the char have sparse resources and still the demand for solar systems increases. Even school children come to our office and ask about solar energy. I have three local staff earning a steady income and we are training more young people on the char. And now Jamal, the branch's first technician, tells me he wants to finish twelfth grade so he can qualify as a Shakti field supervisor. The people living on the char see it eroding day by day. And still they invest in solar home systems even though the solar panel may outlive the char.

"No, I don't think branch managers should have to stay on this char for more than a year. But I seriously believe they can learn for a lifetime while they are here."

Innovations for Ashtamir Char

While the solar program was progressing, Shakti found new ways to improve the livelihoods of the islanders. It began by developing a livestock program and disbursing loans for oxen, buffalo, and sheep, and for high-yield dairy cows, which give up to fifteen liters of milk per day. Dairy cow owners earned money by selling the milk for 25 Taka per liter and could later sell or keep the calves.

Shakti also gave farmers the option of buying young oxen and fattening them until they fetched a good price at the market. An agricultural expert was hired to develop high-yielding grass, which grows fast and feeds more cattle to speed up the process. To help keep the cattle healthy, Shakti added a veterinarian. He advised farmers on how to enrich the fodder with molasses, straw, urea, and rice. Both programs met with success, and Shakti began working on ways to use cow manure for biogas plants on the char.

Shakti engineers constructed six biogas plants for demonstration at no cost to monga-affected families and provided them with cows in exchange for the organic fertilizer produced by the biogas plant. The idea was to market the fertilizer to char farmers, which could later generate income for the owners of the biogas plant. Poor families had the further advantage of cooking with biogas instead of with the grass needed to feed their cattle.

To test the innovation, engineers constructed six biogas plants for *monga*-affected families on the mainland and followed the same model: Shakti supplied enough cows to feed the bio digester in exchange for the fertilizer. These demonstration projects taught Shakti what it could realistically expect from poor families in the crisis area, as well as how the poor could earn an income and build up assets. They also created interest among farmers in the rest of the community for Shakti's newly introduced biogas technology.

To step up the program, Shakti hired a civil engineer for its regional office in Kurigram to supervise all biogas plant construction and maintenance. He was also responsible for training local masons to create local employment. All things considered, Shakti had reason to take an optimistic view of its initial progress with solar and biogas programs in a crisis area. But very little is certain on a char. "Oh, there is a very good chance our biogas plants won't function long-term on a sandy char," claimed the civil engineer. "We'll just have to come up with a better model."

Table 15. Installations Made by the Branch on Ashtamir Char

Year	Solar Home System	Biogas System	Improved Cooking Stove	Comment
2007	79	0	4	Started pilot project for clay cooking stoves
2008	99	6	0	Started pilot project for biogas plants
2009	170	0	0	Shakti branch office washed away by flood.
2010	224	0	5	Concrete cooking stoves introduced
Total	**572**	**6**	**9**	

Table 15 shows the engineer's assumptions turned out to be true. Seasonal floods and sandy soil impeded the construction of the biogas plants and the program ended with the pilot project. Shakti's improved cooking stove met with a similar fate, since the silt and sand were not suited for building a solid stove. But this is not the end of Shakti's work on the char. On the contrary, these setbacks challenge Shakti to innovate.

Its sturdy new stove model made of concrete is a promising alternative to the clay stove for households on the char. It is inexpensive, saves on fuel and comes ready-made from Shakti's stove production center in Kurigram. Shakti has started a tree cultivation program and is experimenting with new biogas plant models better suited for a char.

And yet, Shakti cannot ignore the realities of life on Ashtamir Char. Its entire community town square was washed away during seasonal flooding in 2009. Shakti, the Grameen Bank branch, the schools and other organizations have all relocated further inland to continue their work. Chilmari, the once famous river port during the Pakistani and British Rule, has been washed away by the Bramaputra-Jamuna River. And still, life goes on. Shakti's challenge is to make it a better life for the people on Ashtamir Char.

The river erodes one bank and builds another. That's the play of the river.
Bangladeshi Proverb

Cultivating Engineers to Reach Millions

Shakti's engineers, who pioneered solar systems in 1997, learned on the job, from suppliers, customers, and from each other. Often stationed alone for months in rural areas, they were glad to share their know-how and quickly brought novice colleagues up to speed. Shakti progressed at its own slow pace, village by village, and didn't need to worry about staffing and training. These issues came into focus in 2001, when the company was about to install 13,000 solar systems. Shakti then needed specialists for batteries and charge controllers and managers for procurement and production, and they favored engineers to do the job.

To this day, Shakti's business depends on engineers. True, engineers want career perspectives, nice offices, and good salaries. Technicians work for less. But engineers are all-around experts, invaluable assets to a fast-growing company.

Engineers handle more demanding workloads and more complex problems than semiskilled technicians. They're good troubleshooters and can design good products. When Shakti introduced improved cooking stoves, engineers observed how customers used them, what the problems were, and modified the design accordingly. Rural customers demand first-class service in return for their hard-earned money and trust in engineers.

But most important to Shakti as it rapidly expands field operations is that engineers excel as trainers. They understand the technology *and* the market and quickly bring their branch trainees up to standard. Shakti's future success will depend on a corps of qualified engineers in the field as it embarks upon major growth.

Training for Growth

Most of the sixty-four districts in Bangladesh have engineering institutes. At a polytechnic institute, a student receives the degree of Diploma Engineer; at a university a Bachelor of Science (BSc) degree in engineering. Renewable energy technologies, however, are still a new field of study, and most engineers have little expertise in this field when Shakti hires them. Nor are they always the natural energy emissaries the organization needs to relate well to village customers. Shakti has to cultivate its own corps of engineers.

Engineers begin their training with an introductory seminar at the head office in Dhaka. Then they are sent to a branch. It would be naïve to assume that every newly hired Shakti engineer eagerly awaits going to the villages.

They often don't know what to expect or how they will fare. But they will soon find this out.

Branch managers waste no time when introducing trainees to their new job. They test their initiative, encourage them to take on demanding tasks, and even ask them for suggestions on how they would improve branch operations. They take them along on their daily trips to the market; introduce them to customers and village leaders. "Some trainees can't cope with walking long hours without a timetable," explains a branch manager. "Others have difficulty adjusting to village life in an unfamiliar region. They do satisfactory work in the office and with the technology, but can't relate to the customer. This is exactly what we need to find out during training. As future managers, they can't run the branch from behind an office desk."

Although trainees are guided through their first system installations, they are soon held responsible for their work. If a trainee forgets one of the fifty items needed to install a solar system—say 10 kilometers down the road—he must return and fetch the equipment. If he confuses the customer with theoretical explanations, is impatient or impolite, he is admonished.

Branches are never overstaffed and therefore welcome quick learners and helping hands. When off the job, trainees live, eat, and interact with all staff members at the mess, the living quarters near the branch. It is an intense learning experience. And those who stay on will be glad for it when they are later on their own.

A Training Company

Engineers sign a three-year contract with Grameen Shakti when they are hired, which specifies their training allowance and salary. In most cases, a trainee can become a branch manager within six months. Roughly 36 percent of engineer trainees are not suited for the job, and they usually find this out during training and leave on their own accord. Some of them later return for a second try.

Training in the field puts everything into sharp perspective: trainees' initiative, how they relate to village customers and village life, teamwork, discipline, and service. For those who have a tough time in the field, it's better to detect this early. The training process is all the more important because the trainees will later train others. But they can't teach, nor can they delegate, what they have not learned themselves.

By 2008, Shakti had 400 branches. If one engineer trained another at each branch, 400 engineers could be trained in six months, about 800 within one year, which would keep pace with the company's expansion. Shakti's branches thus function like a virtual academy and a natural training camp. "In a rural service company like Shakti, you have to train everyone," explains a senior manager, "the engineers, the technicians, the customers. In a sense, we're a training company."

Job Rotation

A manager usually stays no more than three years at any one branch. After a few years in one place, they tend to get settled, put down roots, and relax. Then the time has come for them to move around in the company, to acquire new tasks and responsibilities.

Depending on their experience, branch managers may be transferred to another branch or promoted to manage a region. A different branch means unfamiliar terrain, new people, and new challenges. For those who become regional managers, it means the supervision of six to ten branch offices and monthly trips to the head office in Dhaka.

Promotion to divisional manager is the next major step. In 2008, there were seven divisional managers, all of whom had pioneered Shakti's first branches and later served as regional managers. One manager recalls his promotion to divisional manager:

"Moving to Chittagong was a dramatic experience for me. No one in my entire family had ever been this far south. Chittagong was already a huge division in 2008, with eight regional offices, stretching over 200 kilometers from the Hill Tracts in the north to seven islands in the Bay of Bengal in the south. Everything was different—the food, the dialects, the people, the terrain. Water was everywhere. But the biggest difference was that I was challenged to supervise fifty branches with 30,000 customers.

"Gone were the days when as branch manager I made daily visits to the busy bazaars I so enjoyed and friendly customers greeted me by name. As regional manager I had six branches to supervise, but visited them a few times a month and phoned them every day. Now, it was all about numbers, controlling, checking and decisions, accounting and reporting—but I still made time for personal visits to the branches. Why? Because the branches are the heart of Grameen Shakti. If they have a problem, so do I.

"Once a new branch manager in a remote Hill Tract area feared collecting installments because he thought it too dangerous. I traveled 100 kilometers to his branch and went out with him into the villages to visit his customers. I did this for days until the branch manager felt confident he could do it alone. Even as divisional manager, it's my job to support the branch because this is where you learn. Village people taught me everything. When I left the village, it was like leaving my birthplace."

The Demands of Expansion

By 2008, recruiting had become a critical activity. It was not difficult during Shakti's first years, when many engineers were unemployed in Bangladesh. The respected Grameen name and the appeal of a new technology attracted good candidates, and Shakti hired them if certain conditions were met. The ideal applicant was an engineer by education; less than twenty-eight years of age; not previously employed; willing to live, work, and rough it in rural areas; and able to make an appealing presentation to the customer.

Shakti still looks for branch engineers who are physically fit and can communicate well. But as the organization rapidly expands its branch operations, Shakti has begun hiring young villagers with twelve years of schooling as field supervisors in addition to engineers. This makes sense after a decade of business. Now handbooks exist and experienced branch staff is on hand to guide the trainees. They need not be as qualified as the early engineers, who had to invent techniques and bootstrap the business.

Moreover, as with the local technicians, field supervisors learn technical skills and earn a steady income, which is part of what Shakti set out to do in the first place: to provide income opportunities and renewable energy to rural communities.

Hiring Field Supervisors

When searching for talent, Shakti relies on its good reputation and the finesse of its field management. Regional and divisional managers look for promising field supervisors in their districts. Shakti advertises for jobs in local and national newspapers and keeps in contact with vocational schools for prospective candidates. Shakti's interviewing committee comprises both field and head office managers, but they interview prospective field supervisors at the divisional offices to save them the expensive trip to Dhaka.

"Hundreds apply," a human resource manager explains. "Most applicants come from farmers' families, so when I asked one applicant if he could carry a 40 kg battery and walk 10 kilometers to reach a remote village, he responded by showing me his hands. 'Look, they are calloused from hard work,' he said.

'Heavy loads are nothing new to me.' Another young man told us his father was a businessman. He looked like he came from a poor family, so we asked what his father's business might be. 'A rickshaw puller,' he answered. As it turned out this applicant had helped pulling his father's rickshaw for years as a young boy, and still had the drive to complete twelve years of schooling and pass his exams. We hired both applicants."

"What counts in the long term is character," adds a divisional manager. "A branch depends on teamwork and each member of the team must be willing to walk that extra mile to do his job well. If the branch doesn't function, neither does my division." Shakti looks for young people who show initiative and a will to contribute. As employees, they are rewarded with excellent training, a secure job, and ample opportunity for promotion. They are motivated by working on a good team, healthy competition with their young colleagues, and the difference they can make in their communities.

This may be difficult to understand for people who didn't grow up in an energy-starved country like Bangladesh. But for the many Shakti engineers and technicians who grew up in villages with broken-down generators, dim lighting, and acute energy shortage every day, this is a chance for change. As Shakti engineers and technicians, they can apply their knowledge of renewables to help overcome the harsh reality of their families and communities.

Keeping the Rural Network Intact

By 2007, Shakti had become a highly decentralized rural organization with more than 400 field offices distributed all over the country. Travel was a major strain on divisional managers who had to transport batteries, panels, and equipment to their branches and bring back broken parts for repair. This was even more difficult to keep up when the branch network expanded to fifty branches in one division, since field offices were poorly connected by roads. Shakti's field operations and closely-knit network were at risk.

To remedy the problem, all divisional managers were provided with a pick-up truck and driver. This was costly and a major decision during expansion when Shakti was already opening eight branches a month. But improved transport was necessary to keep divisional managers in close contact with their branches and to expedite the flow of equipment. Anything that facilitates travel and communication in rural Bangladesh is of import to Shakti's business.

At the branch level, Shakti provides its branch managers and staff with low-interest loans to buy motorcycles in addition to a travel allowance for fuel. Branch managers in particular enjoy the time saved on travel to attend to their duties at the branch office. However, management is reconsidering this decision because of frequent motorcycle accidents. Traveling rough village terrain is risky, and branch managers all too often forget to wear their helmets. Other hazards persist. Thieves trapped a branch manager on a mountain road in the Hill Tracts and stole his motorcycle. "So many branch managers want a motorcycle," comments a senior manager, "but we don't approve the loan until we are sure they are aware of the risks involved and will act responsibly. Otherwise our company travel incentives don't make sense."

Mobile phones are less problematic and help keep the network intact. Shakti provides its employees with a no-interest loan to purchase a mobile phone with two years to repay, plus free SIM cards with a fixed budget for calls. This keeps the branch network in close communication, in addition to saving time and money on travel. By 2007, the majority of Shakti's customers had access to a mobile phone.

But Shakti wouldn't be the company it is, if it didn't think up ways to use its investments for marketing. Divisional managers' pick-up trucks, which are highly visible when driving through thousands of villages, bear Shakti's motto in large letters on the side of the truck: *Solar Power—Better Life—Better Income.*

Keeping Qualified Personnel

Shakti encourages its employees to save money. If a staff member saves 10 percent of his or her basic salary, the company doubles the amount and deposits it in its *Provident Fund* at a commercial bank to earn interest. The fund is administered by an independent board, so only employees have access to their savings.

Shakti's employees also enjoy *gratuity*, which is generous by Bangladeshi standards. After having served the company for five years, staff members are eligible for voluntary retirement and entitled to a gratuity worth five times the amount of their last month's (basic) salary. Another popular option among employees is *earned leave*, the trading of time for money. An employee receives three days earned leave for every month of service. After a minimum of three years, an employee can cash in one month's earned leave and get one month's salary in return.

Group life insurance was introduced in 2007, whereby Shakti pays a monthly premium for each staff member to an insurance company. In case of death, the employee's family receives prompt financial assistance according to salary and organizational status. The *Staff Welfare Fund* to provide financial assistance in case of accident or illness was established in 2008.

Shakti motivates its employees with additional advantages. They enjoy a bonus equivalent to one month's basic salary for each of the two Eid festivals held during the year, a pay scale raise every five years, allowances for inflation, and ample opportunities to move up in a fast-growing company.

A popular event among Shakti's staff is the company-sponsored annual family picnic. Branch staff hires a cook, rents electronic audio equipment, creates branch banners, and hires a bus for transportation to wherever they want to celebrate. Employees at all levels of management compete in athletics and family games, and the winners are awarded with prizes.

All of the above conveys one important message to company employees: Shakti cares. It wants every member of its staff and its families to benefit from a secure job in all situations of life. Jobs which are highly valued but rare in developing countries, jobs which attract, motivate, and keep qualified personnel.

One New Branch a Day

In 2007, Shakti was scaling up operations to install one million solar systems by 2015. With 1,500 engineers and technicians, and only 340 branches, it did not appear as though Shakti could achieve such an ambitious goal. But Shakti had a plan. The more qualified staff it trained, the faster it could expand. During the next three years, Shakti would increase its workforce by a factor of six to 9,000 employees. While Shakti was opening eight branches a month in 2007, it would be opening one branch a day in 2010.

The following sections describe how Shakti developed into the largest off-grid rural solar energy provider in the world. The challenges it faced on its steep path of expansion were immense. Shakti would need to train thousands of engineers and technicians; it would need battery and computer specialists, as well as experts in accounting, finance, and procurement. As the organization decentralized operations from the head office to the villages, it needed qualified personnel in rural areas, which were hard to come by even in Dhaka. Moreover, after going to the expense of training its field staff, Shakti would be hard pressed to keep it as new solar providers entered the market.

But Shakti also had reason to be optimistic as it prepared for major growth. Its finances were in order, it had an experienced and motivated workforce and its market was booming. "No one has ever done this for the rural people," says a divisional manager. "When I took the job in 1997, I thought solar is a new technology with a big future rural Bangladesh. Now it's actually happening and I'm part of it."

A Storm Called Sidr

In November 2007, Barisal was Shakti's largest division: its seventy-two branches provided solar services to more than 20,000 customers in the Ganges River Delta. One of the division's regional managers, Mr. Razzak, was preparing for a meeting with his branch managers as radio reports continually upgraded the force with which a storm called Sidr was expected to hit the coast of Barisal in southern Bangladesh.

The managers were planning to meet at the branch in Kakchira, about 35 kilometers from the Bay of Bengal, but by early evening on November 14, everything had changed. Storm warnings were blaring from radios, TVs, loudspeakers on mosques, megaphones in rickshaws—all ordering people into cyclone shelters. When the storm signals reached danger Level 10, ferry services were halted across the coastal region, and fishing boats were warned to return to shore. Barisal was alerted to prepare for the worst.

Razzak phoned each of his six branch managers and instructed them to take the solar panels from their office roofs, secure batteries and store-room supplies, put all ledgers and records in the Almirah—the office metal cabinet—and, where possible, help customers safeguard their solar systems. Branch staff informed their customers by phone, some of the local technician set out on foot. Razzak recalled the storm.

"I was especially concerned about the new branch manager in Kakchira. He had been manager of this branch for only two months, was twenty-five years old, still inexperienced, and came from a district unaffected by the cyclonic storms of the coastal region. If Sidr struck as violently as predicted, his branch office on the river Bishkhali so close to the coast would be in serious danger. My divisional manager, Mr. Mukhlasur, strongly advised me not to take this risk, but I was certain the new branch manager would need my help and decided to start out early the next morning for Kakchira.

"My journey began at 6.30 a.m. at the bus station and a three-hour-wait for a bus which never came. Clearly, bus drivers were heeding government warnings and not traveling south at all that day. I hired a motorcycle to take me part of the way, traveled the last 8 kilometers by rickshaw and managed to arrive in Kakchira shortly before noon. I received a hearty welcome from the branch manager and learned that his local technician—his only staff person as a new branch manager—was out in the villages helping customers prepare for the storm.

"We immediately went to work at the branch office; taking down the ceiling fan and placing the office ledgers in the six-foot-high Almirah. The office was housed on the ground floor of a two-storied brick building and seemed like a safe-enough place. But it was hard for us to ignore the loud blasts of wind against the windows. I thought up jobs to keep us busy, and was never so glad for my mobile phone."

On the evening of November 15, Cyclone Sidr reached peak winds of 260 km/h and made landfall near the mangrove forests, setting off driving rains in its path. It first struck the southern-most villages on the coastline of Barisal in Patharghata, where it took out hundreds of homes that had been built on the slope of a long embankment. In its wake, a five-meter tidal wave wiped out entire villages. The force of the tidal wave was so strong that it demolished brick mosques. Winds blew furiously as the eye of the cyclone neared the confluence of the Baleshwar and Bishkhali, pushing the swollen rivers inland as it cut its destructive swath toward Kakchira.

"The power failed around 6 p.m. Fortunately, the owner of our building lived on the floor above the branch office and had a 40W solar home system. It powered three lamps, including a light outside which people could see from a distance. Villagers soon began pouring in for shelter, soaking wet and scared. I was worried about how I could manage when things got worse and where the local technician might be stranded. He had not yet returned to the branch.

"The winds increased in intensity and were so loud I could hardly hear my divisional manager on my mobile. I had just managed to shout into the phone that the tin roof had been blown off the house, when my phone went dead. The only thing my mobile could do now was show me the time. It was 8 p.m.

"Incredibly, villagers were still braving the storm to find refuge in our building. The upstairs room was about 900 square feet with now over 200 villagers crowded into it. When space became a problem, I told everyone to allow all women and children to remain upstairs and for the men to come down to the ground floor. Most of the tin roof was gone, but the building's wooden frame and the wooden ceiling beneath it were holding. The battery was charged and the wiring intact. Despite all the chaos around us, we had light. It seemed to calm people. All was not lost.

"But for how long? The wind flattened the small building housing the kitchen next door and smashed it onto the side of our house. We were still safe inside, but the unrelenting winds were like ambulance sirens next to my head. My only thought now was to keep everyone calm—including myself.

"At 11 p.m., the Bishkhali River poured over its banks flooding the already leveled bazaar and the ground floor of our house. In minutes the water was up to my knees, slowly inching its way up to my waist. I tried to keep a clear head, debating if and when we would need to go outside if the water kept rising. I had kept all three doors on the ground floor closed, but now opened the door to the north side (as the strongest winds were coming from the south), to check the conditions outside. There was a heavy current, and I could hardly believe my eyes when I saw a woman clutching a baby to her breast and carrying a bundle of belongings in her hand. I called to her to come into the house, but she couldn't hear me and seemed to be in shock. I waded out to help her and could see that the baby in her arms was dead. She had been standing on a piece of ground higher than our office and it took all my strength to move her safely through the water and into the building. I led her still holding her baby to the crowded staircase and could see there was still light upstairs.

"The water kept rising. What would I do when water reached my neck? What if people panicked? I was on automatic pilot—looking for damaged equipment, checking my mobile for the time, wondering why the water was so warm. I made my way upstairs to see if the battery was still safe and found its owner, Mr. Tipu, guarding it. Miraculously, the solar lamp was still burning. And two young girls had made it to safety in our house, despite the strong river current.

"My mobile displayed 12.45 a.m. when the winds finally calmed. With water up to my chest, I felt a huge sense of relief as the Bishkhali River rapidly receded and Cyclone Sidr diminished into a tropical storm. In took less than an hour for the water to drain from the office. We had survived. Now there was work to do.

"At 3 a.m., the local technician returned to the office in his underwear, carrying his soaked trousers and shirt. He had been helping a customer and was unable to make it back to the branch before Sidr hit. But as a native to the area, he knew about a concrete mosque where he and many others had found safety. We discussed what was to be done after daybreak, and how we could find out what had happened to our branch colleagues further south near the Bay of Bengal, since communications were down. I decided to risk the journey to the Patharghata branch office—about 16 kilometers south of Kakchira—on foot. Located near the confluence of two rivers and so close to the sea, this branch would have suffered the full brunt of the cyclone. At 5 a.m., I set out for the branch.

"What I saw on the way was overwhelming. The roads had craters that looked like they had been made by meteorites and were blocked by fallen trees and power-lines. Boats from the river had been washed away by the cyclone and stranded on the roads. Patharghata had effectively been cut off from the rest of the world. I couldn't pass through—not even on foot. I had to turn back.

"My 20-kilometer-trek north to my regional office took hours, but I was glad to recognize enough of the road to get there. A few kilometers from my office in Mothbaria I managed to hire a motorcycle; and after an incredible day filled with the sight of devastation, I returned to an office building fully intact and branch staff members overjoyed to see me. No one was injured. I couldn't speak, I was so grateful. After all I had been through in only forty-eight hours; it was as though I had been given a second life."

In Sidr's Wake

In fewer than ten hours, Cyclone Sidr had destroyed much of the densely populated coastal area of Bangladesh. It was the strongest cyclone to hit the country since 1991, when one of the deadliest tropical cyclones on record killed nearly 140,000 people.

Sidr was no less severe than the 1991 cyclone, but early warning systems plus the building of cyclone shelters and embankments had greatly reduced the fatalities. Although Sidr had claimed fewer than 4,000 lives, the damage to homes, crops, and family livelihoods was immense. Sidr had literally flattened houses made of thatch, wood, tin, and even brick; smashed fishing trawlers; killed livestock; and flooded once prosperous shrimp farms.

This was not the first time branch staff members had experienced floods and disaster, but it was the first time they had been in the path of a major cyclone. In Sidr's wake, they faced problems far different from repairing a solar system: which customers to visit first, what equipment to carry, and how to keep track of what the customers needed most. "We all left the next day for the villages, repaired what we could until just before nightfall, when we had to return to the office," recalled Razzak. "It was too dangerous walking the treacherous village roads after dark. "

It was while listening to their customers that branch engineers learned how much more would be needed in the villages than solar repairs. Many customers were in dire financial distress. In the county of Patharghata alone, 75 percent of all households were affected by Sidr. An estimated 150,000 people had lost part or all of their homes, farms, and businesses; many of them couldn't work because they had been injured and thus lost their only source of income. Prior to the storm, the shrimp and *hilsa* fish harvest for Partharghata's large fishing community had been unusually generous. Hilsa, the official national fish of Bangladesh, is of the essence in Bengali cuisine. Fisherman and shrimp farmers were having a good year, and expectations for substantial profits were high. Now, what was a thriving business had been washed away, and entire families faced financial ruin.

Shakti sent a task force from the head office to assist branch staff in assessing the damage. They visited customers and recruited local technicians to help do repairs. Shakti documented customers' financial situation and losses; it stopped collection of installments for at least six months in devastated regions like Patharghata. More problems arose if solar systems had been completely destroyed. With an income of only about 6,000 Taka per month, fishermen could not afford to replace their solar systems. Shakti therefore set about replacing the solar home systems free of charge. The same held true for repairing and replacing solar system components.

But while financial problems could be addressed from the head office in Dhaka, it was the branch engineers and technicians who experienced firsthand the emotional toll on village people. In Kakchira, where an estimated 400 of its 600 households had suffered catastrophic losses, they experienced people in complete shock. A local technician remembers: "One man asked me if I had seen his children and where his house was. The whole market in Kakchira had been totally run into the ground. Roads had disappeared. Nothing looked familiar except for the Bishkhali River."

In Sarankhola, where Sidr had laid waste to entire villages and once-flourishing shrimp farms, branch members described the grim aftermath of the storm: "People simply could not grasp the harsh reality that they had lost everything in only a few hours. What do you say to a customer who has lost all four of his children? This was an altogether new experience for us at the branch. We took time to talk to the village people. This seemed to help."

Shakti was not alone in offering assistance to Sidr victims. Government relief teams, aid organizations, and hundreds of volunteers made a huge effort to bring relief to the cyclone disaster areas. But bringing relief to villages that Razzak couldn't even get to on foot posed insurmountable problems. For weeks, villages in Patharghata could be reached only by air or by boat from the Bay of Bengal. The Shakti branch office building in Patharghata, however, had miraculously survived the cyclone, and branch engineers and technicians were out helping village people only hours after the storm.

This was no exception. Shakti runs dozens of branches in the communities hardest hit by Sidr, where branch staff worked to the limit to help village people when they needed it most. Incredibly, Mr. Razzak and the branch staff in Mothbaria visited all 400 customers in only three days. "Our customers couldn't believe their eyes when they saw us coming. In villages, which were in complete confusion and disorder, we were already there to help them do repairs."

The Bright Side of Sidr

Shakti had resourceful managers and a technology so reliable it could function during a tropical cyclone. The solar-powered lamp at the branch office in Kakchira burned all through the night until 6 a.m. the next morning. Shakti would later learn how solar lamps had saved lives in hundreds of villages on the delta.

While many branches converted their offices into emergency cyclone shelters, it was their bright solar lamps that guided villagers to safety while Sidr raged. When the town, Patuakhali, was under six feet of water more than 500 people fled to Shakti's regional office, whose 75W solar system illuminated all three floors of the building. Resourceful branch engineers in Kaukhali, whose office had no solar system, hooked up a battery to two lamps from the storeroom and mounted them outside the office to light up the building and the road in front of it. As the Baleshwar River flooded the villages, more than 700 people were able to find their way to safety in the sturdy branch office building on higher ground.

Shakti's solar services were no less significant after Sidr had passed. The town of Patuakhali, for example, didn't have grid electricity for almost three weeks. To recharge their mobile phones, people came to Shakti's regional office in town; many made visits to branch offices and village customers. Branch engineers also supplied outdoor camps for homeless Sidr victims with solar systems to power lamps, radios, and mobile phones. For people still in shock and literally cut off from the rest of the world, it meant a lot to be able to communicate with their families when the mobile phone network came to life again.

In the midst of disaster, thousands of people experienced the *power* of solar electricity—literally—when solar-powered lamps and mobile chargers were the only ones working. Afterward, when people had recovered from the shock, the demand for solar energy grew substantially on the delta. Patharghata, where three quarters of the population had suffered severe losses, would later become Shakti's most successful region in Barisal, with more than 9,000 customers.

In the weeks following Sidr, branch staff replaced a total of 150 solar panels and repaired 2,000 solar systems in Barisal Division. Shakti provided this service free of charge to its customers to help them recover their losses. It also would have to work on a disaster contingency plan to minimize future company losses. The low-lying delta remains highly vulnerable to tropical storms, and there is no logic as to when, where, or how hard cyclones will strike next.

But Shakti had also learned what worked; why the company functioned so well during a catastrophic cyclone. Branch engineers and technicians lived and worked in the villages devastated by the cyclone. They were young and physically fit. They knew where mosques were located for shelter; they could walk for 20 kilometers in regions where roads and markets had disappeared and still find their way to their destinations. Village customers and their neighbors knew and trusted Shakti staff and welcomed them as friends when they came to do repairs. Branch staff, on the other hand, not only made a personal effort to help their customers when they needed it most. As engineers and technicians, they could repair the solar systems, recruit locals, and train them to help out.

In the aftermath of the cyclone, Shakti had a network of field offices in place to support its staff and to keep head office managers informed. This made quick decisions and prompt disaster relief possible, such as supplying the camps with solar power, providing financial assistance for severe losses, panel replacement and system repairs. The positive lesson Cyclone Sidr so clearly revealed to everyone at Grameen Shakti is what worked: an operational rural network, a trained and proactive staff, and social engineers committed to people

Coastline endangered by storms

Off the Shelf Won't Sell

Shakti does business in three main areas: solar systems, biogas plants, and improved cooking stoves. This is a common product spectrum in developing countries. Trade fairs on renewables worldwide abound with products of this type. Yet, systems that have sold a hundred thousand times in the industrialized world would not sell in Bangladesh and vice versa. Solar home systems, so very popular with Shakti's customers, would hardly become a sales hit in a developed country.

Shakti's products are specialized to the needs of the rural population in a poor developing country. Product design balances demands on usability, cost and procurement, repair and maintenance. It embodies years of experience.

Shakti has marketed solar systems since 1996 in various configurations it calls *packages*. A package combines components into a system to serve a certain type of use. Packages are used in homes and offices, at bazaars, on fishing boats and vendor carts, for telecommunication base stations. The Appendix describes about two dozen packages, solar home systems in particular. They enjoy great popularity in Bangladesh.

A solar home system package normally consists of a photovoltaic (PV) module, also called solar panel, which generates electricity from sunlight; a battery to store the electricity during the day; and a charge controller to regulate the charging and discharging of the battery. It feeds loads like lamps, TV, radios, mobile phone chargers, fans, and appliances.

Although the components of a package are well balanced, a good deal of customer training is needed to keep the systems running. Entire families—all users of the system—are warned about the dangers of fire or explosive products near the battery. They are taught not to cover the battery with polythene and to understand why each lamp, radio, and TV should be connected directly with the battery terminals. If the terminals of the battery are found to be loose, Shakti should be contacted. If the specific gravity of the battery fluid becomes less than 1170, then the battery should rest for a minimum of three days and charged without using any load. In times of flood, the battery should be placed on high ground or on the rafters just under the roof. In case of a cyclone forecast, the solar panel should be taken down. Under no circumstances should anyone replace the fuse of the charge controller.

These are the company's rules for maintenance as they are printed in the Customer Instruction Manual, but Shakti does far more to educate its customers. The rules also are taught in user trainer sessions and explained again by branch staff on its monthly visits to customers. By 2010, Shakti had trained more than 200,000 solar system users in the maintenance of their systems. In Shakti's early years, customers were so well trained by its pioneering engineers that some batteries lasted for thirteen years, the panels, charge controllers, and wiring still intact. In times of disaster like Cyclone Sidr, branch staff phoned hundreds of customers and personally went out into the villages to help them safeguard their solar systems.

Customer know-how is as important to rural business as a good product. When Shakti learned that customers let their batteries run all the way to empty while watching a good movie, it had to come up with a better way to educate its customers. It equipped branch offices with battery recharging gear and recharged customers' batteries for free—but only for the first time this happened. It worked. Customers understood that with proper care, the life cycle of a battery is up to eight years even though the warranty is only for five. They save money if they don't turn off the charge controller.

Though solar home systems make up the bulk of the solar business, Shakti also installs a variety of more powerful systems. 6 kW and 7 kW systems for base stations for telecommunications were installed in Sylhet and on the Bay of Bengal. To withstand strong winds and storms, they are anchored in cement and equipped with lightning rods. All are hybrid systems, which have reduced diesel generators' running time from about ten to two hours per day. On sunny days, to zero.

In Dhaka, Shakti has installed a few hybrid solar systems with grid connection as back-ups for restaurants and private households. The potential market in a megacity plagued with load shedding and power outages is enormous. But the cost of a solar system is still high when compared to an instant power system as a back-up. This is still the cheaper and preferred solution in urban areas connected to the grid.

Business with Biogas

Shakti waited almost a decade before introducing biogas technology. Engineers recognized early on its potential in an agrarian economy and experimented with several models, but initial investments for biogas plants remained high both for the customer and for the company. After working out a customer financing model and with a strong solar market to build on, Shakti introduced biogas plants to commercial poultry, fish and dairy farms as well as to private households in 2005. They produce gas for cooking, lighting and for generators to produce electricity.

Biogas plants use conventional technology and can be built by trained masons using local materials. They are constructed underground, wasting little space. They digest organic waste such as cow dung, poultry litter, and crop wastes and destroy bacteria and viruses in the process. If properly operated, a biogas plant produces gas continuously. The cost of construction can be recovered within two to three years, and it can function for twenty-five years.

Among the various types of biogas plants, Shakti opted for the fixed-dome model as illustrated in the Appendix. Special care must be taken when choosing the construction site, since it should be on firm plain land distant from rivers or canals. The site should be protected from flood, open to the sun, distant from tree roots that could crack the plant, and close to the source of dung and organic waste needed to feed the digester.

The fact that farm owners no longer had to bear the cost of waste disposal turned out to be a popular feature of biogas plants. Farmers could collect animal waste from inside the barn, channel it directly into the digester, and use the gas produced to generate the electricity to light the barn. Farmers also saved on chemical fertilizer, since the organic residue from the biogas plant could be used to fertilize vegetables and rice fields, and to feed fish.

Private households likewise valued a clean living environment free of insects swarming about food waste outside the house, since the refuse could now be fed into the biogas plant. Biogas, like natural gas, burns without smoke, and families enjoy healthier, smoke-free kitchens. Families further benefit from savings on firewood and liquefied petroleum gas used for cooking, which is perhaps the best understood advantage of biogas.

Investment into biogas plants can be recovered through savings on firewood or fuel, and in future through earnings from organic fertilizer. A biogas plant fed with 130 kg of dung (and water) can render 4.8 m^3 of biogas, in addition to 40 to 45 kg of dry organic fertilizer. This could become a promising business for biogas plant owners, which Shakti's agricultural experts are working to develop in order to reduce farmers' dependency on chemical fertilizer.

Business with Bio Slurry

Although chemical fertilizer is produced in Bangladesh, more than 2.5 million tons of fertilizer had to be imported to meet farmers' growing needs in 2010. During the past decade alone, Bangladesh's fertilizer imports increased by up to 70 percent. The government controls both production and imports of urea fertilizer, which it distributes through appointed dealers. "And that's just the problem," explains Shakti's agricultural expert, Dr. M.S. Islam.

"The dealers do not always provide a sufficient amount of fertilizer to the farmers when they need it. This mismatch of supply and demand and poor marketing channels are threatening farmers' livelihoods and food security in the country.

"The situation becomes even more serious with the shifts of food surplus countries from export of food to biofuel production. I'm convinced bio slurry has great market potential in Bangladesh, because farmers so desperately need it to increase crop productivity. In an agricultural country like Bangladesh, the fertility of its soil is its most important resource."

The problem is that soil fertility in Bangladesh is steadily deteriorating due to the overuse of chemical fertilizers to grow more food for an ever-increasing population. Soil acidity is high, and the organic matter in soils—the storehouse of plant nutrients—is alarmingly low. If farmers are to increase crop productivity, there is no alternative but to enrich soils with organic fertilizer.

This is a problem bio slurry could help overcome. The bio slurry produced from the organic residue of biogas plants contains 20 to 30 percent more nutrients than commonly used organic fertilizers, such as cow dung, poultry manure, or compost. Findings at Dhaka University and the Bangladesh Agricultural Research Institute show that bio slurry reduces soil erosion, soil acidity, and water loss, while increasing the efficiency of chemical fertilizers. Bio slurry has further advantages for farmers and private households, since it can feed fish and helps grow cereals, oil crops, vegetables, and flowers, spices, and indoor and outdoor plants.

This opens up a promising market for the organic fertilizer produced by biogas plants. The challenge is how to get such a useful product to the user. In order to market bio slurry commercially, it must be collected from the hydraulic chamber of the biogas plant and stored in containers or pits which do not leak and are shielded from rain. Dried slurry then has to be ground, sieved, and packaged before distribution. This is not impossible, but neither is it being done on a large scale.

A business Opportunity for Grameen Shakti Jaibo Shar

In 2007, Shakti launched a program to market bio slurry under the brand name *Grameen Shakti Jaibo Shar*, Grameen Shakti Organic Fertilizer. Everyone can gain. Farmers profit from an abundant supply of organic fertilizer at local markets when they need it and can grow more food; biogas owners have a new source of income and Shakti a new business sector.

Still, the organic fertilizer business is a major undertaking for Shakti. A marketing network must be installed, and dealers must be organized and trained to collect, dry, package, and distribute the fertilizer. A government permit is needed for marketing bio slurry. But Shakti is making good progress.

After testing bio slurry in combination with and without chemical fertilizer, government specialists found that Grameen Shakti Jaibo Shar reduced the use of chemical fertilizer up to 35 percent. As a result, Shakti was granted a government permit to market bio slurry as a commercial product in 2008. Shakti is now working with two rural organizations to market bio slurry. Their job is to collect dried fertilizer from the biogas producers, sieve and package it in bags and to supply local markets. Shakti specialists control the quality.

"So many things have to go right in the beginning", explains Dr. M.S. Islam. We have to train and motivate entrepreneurs and monitor the product. But once they begin earning and farmers see the benefit, the business develops its own dynamic. Bio slurry is now cheaper than urea fertilizer and getting a lot of attention at local markets."

Price Matters

Organic fertilizer will be packaged in 5 kg, 20 kg, and 40 kg quantities and priced at about 10 Taka per kilogram (2010). The cost of urea fertilizer, still widely used in Bangladesh, amounts to about 35 Taka per kilogram, but sells for about 20 Taka per kg due to government subsidies. In the long run, however, government subsidies cannot compensate for the steadily rising price of urea.

Organic fertilizer is thus becoming price competitive without being subsidized. It also will be available in increasing quantities in future, due to the rapid growth of the poultry and livestock industry in Bangladesh. The Bangladesh Department of Livestock Services (DLS) estimates that 200,000 poultry farms could construct biogas plants by 2015.

The Search for a New Model

Much is in the making, but still more is in a state of flux. Thousands of biogas plants have been constructed in Bangladesh by different organizations with different models. Biogas technology has not settled yet, despite the fact that it was introduced in Bangladesh as early as 1972. At that time the floating dome model with steel gas holder was in practice. In 1992, fixed dome plants took over, inspired by a Chinese model. But the search for a suitable model continues for good reasons.

The fixed dome model has inherent disadvantages. Its construction takes fifteen to twenty days, and earthwork is impossible in many areas during monsoon rains. Groundwater or sediments can enter the plant causing problems. It's not leak-proof: up to 20 percent of the gas can escape from the digester. When cattle die or farms are sold, the plant can't be moved to a new location. Moreover, some biogas plant features are disputed. Should expensive galvanized pipes underground or cheaper flexible plastic pipes above ground carry the gas from the place of production to the places of consumption?

Shakti engineers have researched new models since entering the biogas market in 2005. New plant designs, such as plastic tanks were tested and deployed; models were developed, which could be constructed year-round and moved to a new location if necessary. But the most promising innovation is fiberglass technology for underground, portable biogas plants.

They can be installed in two to three hours, even during the rainy season. They are leak-proof, more efficient and produce more biogas with less amounts of dung. If the plant owner sells his cows, the plant can be resold; should he move his cow shed away from the biogas plant, the plant can be moved near his livestock. Shakti can uninstall the biogas plant should its owner default on payments, or simply move it to another location in case of river erosion, for example on chars. The company no longer depends on skilled masons, since the plant is prefabricated.

Shakti engineers have conducted pilot projects with the fiberglass model since 2009 and plan to introduce 2 m³ fiberglass bio digesters in 2011. "We'll still offer our customers the larger brick dome digesters, but the fiberglass model has a promising future," explains a biogas specialist. "Fiberglass lasts for more than 50 years. Who knows, maybe a fiberglass digester can last for more than half a century."

Business with Improved Cooking Stoves

Of the three product types Shakti markets, Improved Cooking Stoves (ICS) are the most recent, but well on their way to becoming a flourishing business. Though the technology is simple, the benefits for the rural population seem immense.

Roughly 90 percent of rural households in Bangladesh cook on traditional stoves called *chulas*, fired with solid fuels such as wood, crop residues, and cow dung. A chula usually has its place on the floor inside the house, protected from rain. It's a simple clay construction built over an open fire pit by layering mud until it reaches one to two feet above the floor. An opening in the clay above the fire holds a pot. Another opening at the base serves to fuel the fire.

Generations of village women have cooked on such traditional stoves despite their distinct drawbacks: there is no chimney to vent the smoke, the clay absorbs too much heat and hot gas flows past the pot without heating it. This makes the chula a very inefficient stove and a serious health risk.

Unlike a chula, an improved cooking stove burns wood and other fuel efficiently, includes a chimney to vent the smoke outdoors, and allows cooking with two to three pots simultaneously. Shakti first introduced a stove model made from clay like a chula, but similar to an iron cooking stove by design. It has three levels— ground, middle, and surface—on which the cooking pots are placed. Important is the cast iron grate for the firewood built into the middle level. It allows for air flow underneath the wood and for the ashes to drop through to the ground, where they can be easily removed

Since launching its improved cooking stove program in 2006, Shakti has modified the stove model several times to suit customers' needs. Improved stoves can have one to three mouths, can be built above ground or partly underground to burn cheap straw and leaves in addition to expensive wood. Commercial stoves are adapted to specific demands, for example for guesthouses, tea plantations, Muslim schools (*madrasa*), and restaurants.

Although village cooks benefitted from smoke-free kitchens, saving money was the best understood advantage of improved stoves in the beginning. Shakti offered a family-size improved cooking stove for 700 Taka. In 2007, stove owners could save up to 300 Taka a month on firewood and got a return on their investment in about two months. Many villagers paid for their new stoves in cash. To reach those who couldn't afford cash payment, Shakti offered a loan for 600 Taka with a down payment of 100 Taka and six months' time to repay.

Shakti would have to continue testing its stove model in different regions before finally getting it right for its village customers. But it seemed as though smoke-free village kitchens, savings on firewood and affordable stoves had the makings of a winning model. This, however, would take Shakti another three years to achieve.

To Understand People's Mind-sets, Try to Change Them

Business in rural areas seems straightforward. Solar home systems, small biogas plants, and simple cooking stoves seem to teach a lesson: practical low-tech products plus good service and customer financing are a sure recipe for good business. Adapting technology to village life teaches a different lesson. The idea of biogas technology for rural Bangladesh bloomed already in the 1970s and soon withered. Improved stove models were introduced as alternatives to the chula thirty years ago with marginal success. Rural organizations have since disseminated hundreds of new and improved clay stoves and solar cookers, often free of cost and with special training. All of them met head on with the inertia of the village market for a new kind of stove and a new way to cook.

Stoves failed because they could only be fueled by expensive wood, and not by cheap straw and leaves. Solar cookers, considered by many to be the ideal alternative to the chula, needed up to forty-five minutes to boil water, were not suited for frying food after sundown, and were a problem during the rainy season. Stove technology, however, was not the main problem. Engineers can improve this. The main reason for failure was that when it comes to something as traditional as cooking, people are creatures of habit with unshakable preferences for what and how food should be prepared

This may vary from coastal to tribal regions, from class to class or according to Muslim and Hindu traditions, but all Bangladeshis will agree that food is a serious business on the delta. Religious festivals and family celebrations are unthinkable without milk-based sweets (*misti*). Shakti has customers who have purchased chulas for the sole purpose of preparing traditional sweets.

Alternatives to the chula thus reach deep into village traditions, which for generations have resisted change even when whole families suffer from smoke-filled rooms. A look at how a typical village cook prepares food for her family shows what it means to cook on a traditional chula.

What's in a Chula

In the early morning when Bhulana fires her chula to prepare breakfast for her family, she first removes the ashes with a coconut shell attached to a stick. Squatting on a wooden board on the ground with her sari wrapped tightly round her knees, she then lights the bamboo leaves, cow-dung cakes, and straw she has placed into the fire hole and blows air on the fire with a hollow bamboo pipe to make it burn faster. Within minutes, the smell of burning straw mingles with the pungent odor of cow dung as smoke gradually clouds around Bhulana.

Straw and leaves burn very fast, so Bhulana must squat close to the chula almost the entire time the food is cooking to continually refuel the stove. In the hot climate, food spoils easily, so she must cook at least twice a day, chopping the vegetables and spices while constantly watching the fire. For a typical Bangladeshi late evening meal, this can take up to two hours, while smoke fills every corner of her small house.

Bhulana will tell you: "When I cook, my eyes burn and I cough just like everyone else in the village, since everyone cooks on a chula like mine." She knows that burns and scalds from boiling water or eye injuries from blowing on the fire are painful. But she cares little about the risk of an open fire. A far greater concern for Bhulana is the cost of firewood and the long hours it takes her to collect leaves and brush. These are Bhulana's biggest problems. Coughing and headaches are normal.

Smoke from the chula lingers inside the house for hours while children play and study, while families gather to eat their meals, and while they sleep at night. Little wonder that so many village people suffer from respiratory diseases; the World Health Organization estimates they are the biggest killers of children under five. You would think that these are compelling reasons to favour improved stoves, which vent the smoke outside and improve the energy-efficiency of a traditional chula by 50 percent. And yet, the improved cooking stoves were slow to catch on—not only among poor villagers.

"So many improved stoves were conceived in the heads of engineers, who thought their technical innovations would revolutionize cooking in rural communities," explains a Shakti stove specialist. "But village women weren't ready for a revolution. They just wanted to cook good curry on a chula as generations have done before them."

Curry cooked on a chula is more than food. It stands for a way of life. Urbanites look forward to visiting their village families because "mother will cook tasty food on the chula." Wedding celebrations in Dhaka offer traditional food cooked on a chula as a special treat for the guests. Curry cooked in hot spices and mustard oil on a wood-burning chula is not only delicious. It's a philosophy.

Traditional chula

Improved cooking stove

Getting the Model Right

During its four years of trials, Shakti learned much about its customers and the imperfections of its improved stoves made from clay. The stoves were difficult for village technicians to construct, problematic during seasonal flooding and demanded time-consuming maintenance from branch staff. Together with Dr. Hasan, the pioneer of improved cooking stoves in Bangladesh in the 1980s, Shakti introduced an improved cooking stove made of concrete in 2010 (see Appendix). Improved cooking stove factories were set up throughout Bangladesh to ensure quality and prompt delivery.

The concrete model has distinct advantages over the mud stove: it comes ready-made from the factory and can be installed by village technicians within one or two days. It can be adjusted in height to suit the cooks' way of preparing food and requires less fuel than the improved mud stoves. Shakti keeps the price low: a domestic single-mouth stove sells for 760 Taka with no service charge.

Within a year of launching the new concrete stove, Shakti had increased installations fourfold and set up more than a hundred stove production centers. The improved stove business flourished even in the crisis area.

What made the difference? According to a zonal manager with years of microcredit experience: "So many things, but probably most of all perseverance. We just kept demonstrating to the cooks that our new stove is everything the chula is, but cheaper and better for their health. I first saw this happen with microcredit for income, then solar electricity for light. Now it's happening with improved cooking stoves for smoke-free kitchens.

"I can remember when the Grameen Bank discovered that 20 percent of its borrowers lost everything due to ill health. It took them years to learn to think about their future health. Now we're promoting improved stoves at Grameen Bank center meetings and women are buying. They understand the benefits of a healthier living space for their families. But villagers don't change their ways overnight."

"Mind-sets play strange tricks on us," observes Grameen Bank's founder, Muhammad Yunus. "We see things the way our minds have instructed our eyes to see. Village women thought cooking on a chula meant an open fire and smoke-filled kitchens. Now half a million women are cooking curry on improved stoves in smoke-free kitchens and enjoying it. Shakti has succeeded in changing village mind-sets."

PV-powered guard's house on a fish farm
...thieves beware, I am not sleeping...

5

Keeping the Engine Running

Managing the School of the Practical

In many companies, the audit department checks records and accounts. At Shakti, audit does all this and more. It is an activity of crucial importance for everyone and everything. Without its internal audit, Grameen Shakti would be a different company.

Back in 2000, when Shakti had branch offices in six districts and fewer than 2,000 customers, branch and head office managers were in close contact with each other and knew what was going on in the company. It was still small, and a few accountants could easily handle the financial audit. But by 2003, when Shakti was serving more than twice as many districts and more than 14,000 customers, to know what was going on at the branch level became more challenging. Dozens of engineers had to be hired and trained and new branches staffed. Managers were rotating from one branch office to another every six months, and new staff was taking their place.

Growth strained the entire organization as branches were given more customers and tasks to manage and head office managers more branches to supervise. Regional and divisional offices were installed to supervise field operations. It was a major step. But head office managers still had to know what was actually going on in the field as the company expanded. Until then, the transparency of the organization had largely been a result of direct communication between the head office and the field, and head office managers especially missed the rich first-hand feedback they used to get in the early days. But Shakti's pioneering days were over. Management had to find ways to learn more about what was going on in the company so it could discover problems early enough to handle them. How were the branches adapting to change and expansion? Was branch staff keeping accurate records?

The remedy to this situation was the internal audit. In 2003, Shakti installed the internal audit as an independent department and hired a former Grameen Bank auditor to establish the audit guidelines. It was the right decision at the right time. Shakti's business had always been based on trust, and this would continue. But management also needed to check operations diligently as business increased: solar home system sales were expected to grow by 50 percent in 2004.

The company's future success depended on accurate information at the branch level and Shakti now had the tools to acquire it: guidelines for financial transactions, vouchers, daily transaction books, customer installment cards. More than this, Shakti had a team of auditors ready to implement and check the procedures.

Audits Are Rigorous

At the start when audit had only two teams and a staff of four, it took two years to audit the head office and all branches. By December 2007, Shakti had thirty-two qualified accountants conducting annual audits and was stepping up the pace to a complete company audit every six months. This was achieved in early 2008 when the audit department moved from Dhaka to the divisional offices, where audit teams were closer to the branches and could focus on one division.

Audit teams provide an X-ray of branch operations. They scrutinize every detail, from how long the money collected by employees is kept at a branch office to the cost of a rickshaw when visiting a customer. Spending up to ten days at a branch office, the audit team first checks the Cash-in-hand Register. Regulations require that all collected installments are immediately deposited at the local bank. With the exception of petty cash, not a single Taka is to be kept in the branch office. If staff collects installments in late afternoon or just before the weekend when the bank is closed, then it must record in the Cash-in-hand Register exactly how much cash was kept at the branch for exactly how many days. The Bank Ledger documents the date on which the money was deposited in the bank. The Petty-cash book records all small expenditures.

The audit guidelines are designed to improve branch operations, accounting procedures, and employee performance. In practice, audits do all this and more. They provide Shakti with invaluable feedback from its employees and its customers. "It's not enough just to check the ledgers," an audit team reports. "We're dealing with human beings. We have to read between the lines and listen to everyone. We are sensitive to any difficulties staff members may be having with their colleagues or their customers. We also talk to customers and other people in the village to get their side of the story."

Auditors are highly qualified with a master's degree in accounting. But the internal audit at the branches is more like a school of the practical—guided by experience and observation rather than theory. It leads to practical results. And what could be more practical than understanding how to discover a company's weak points in time to correct them. In the following, audit team members give an account of an unusual case, which demonstrates how their observations and thoroughness work in practice.

"We remember one case in 2006 when we were checking a branch's cash receipts. A cash receipt is issued by branch staff to a customer to document his or her payment. As the receipt is written, a carbon copy is produced for the record. The payment is then recorded in the customer installment card and again in the customer ledger at the branch office.

"We spot-checked about 45 percent of the installment cards to make sure customers' payments had been deposited in the local bank, and discovered that some cash receipts counted for less than what the customer had actually paid. As it turned out, one staff member had simply removed the carbon paper when he wrote the receipt of 3,500 Taka for the customer. Then he reinserted it to forge a carbon copy for 3,000 Taka for the office records. The difference, 500 Taka, went into his pocket.

"We looked to see if this was happening anywhere else and discovered a few others who had risked far more by issuing a cash receipt for 25,000 Taka to the customer and then cancelling it altogether to pocket the entire amount. It is very rare that others at the branch office are involved in such fraud, but it can happen. In one such case last year, staff members cancelled 20 cash receipts at a single branch office. They simply told us that the customers hadn't paid, and were amazed when we found them out."

"And this shows," say experienced head office audit coordinators "why there is a need for unrelenting supervision. Internal audit teams discovered these irregularities in 2006 when we were hiring dozens of new engineers a month and had expanded branch operations to all sixty-four districts in Bangladesh. No matter how well we train them; there will always be people who can't resist the temptation of taking some of the money that passes through their hands. Sometimes it's only little things they feel certain no one will notice: maybe they take a few Taka more than the actual fare for a rickshaw or river boat; or allow a customer to pay for the transport and then take the money from petty cash. Sometimes employees are tempted to take a few meters of cable, or some unused equipment and sell it at the local market."

But whatever the mistake an employee makes, there is a ledger for the audit team to check. They check again when they talk to customers, rickshaw drivers, and staff colleagues. Moreover, should auditors not discover inconsistencies in the cash receipt ledger the first time it's checked, they can re-examine it one to two years later and still claim repayment from staff members if they were at fault. What is important is that every single Shakti employee knows that not even minute details escape the audit teams.

"The chief role of an internal audit is to give guidance and create discipline," explains a senior manager. "We have our rules and expect them to be followed." Auditors, however, have no authority to punish. As a learning organization, Shakti cultivates teamwork, open discussion, and a spirit of inquiry. At the end of the branch audit, the audit team sits together with branch staff and regional and divisional managers to discuss its findings and recommendations. *Mukta alochane*, as it is called in Bangla, is a group discussion, which very often leads to more efficient branch operations and new ideas. It was discussions like these that turned up the first loopholes in the guidelines, which had previously worked so well and now needed improvement. They give branches a chance to rectify old problems and respond to new ones. For this reason, audit teams don't see mistakes as failures, but as chances to improve the company. After detecting cash receipt errors, for instance, audit recommended branch staff use cash receipt pads with carbonless copy paper. It's a safer way to record customer payments. Management took audit's advice and remedied the problem.

"Audit's findings teach us to face the facts," the chief audit co-ordinator adds, "our company can maintain excellence only if it gets honest feedback from its field staff and customers. If, for example, a staff member accounts for travel money to visit a customer's remote house and instead meets the customer at the nearby market, this means much more than taking company money for a trip he didn't make. Far more damaging to our business is that he didn't do his job. Yes, he collected the monthly installment. But he should also have checked and taken care of the customer's solar system. What if the lamps don't work a few days later? If audit doesn't check everything, the customers will. And they may not be so forgiving."

Audit Tools

An auditor's most valuable assets are professional experience and acuity. Because all branch offices are checked, auditors get to know common soft spots and performance indicators. Performance measures inform the company about whether a branch office performs above or below average. Table 16 shows the main topics.

Table 16. Audit Types and Tools

Financial Audit	Performance Audit
• verification of cash transactions	• analysis of implementation of working plan
• verification of customer, bank, and in-stock ledgers	
• verification of the bank balance	• analysis of sales and customer service
• analysis of the trend of expenses	• analysis of expenditures
• analysis of procurement, quantity, price, approval	• analysis of business process efficiency
• analysis of production unit, how much produced etc.	• verification of disciplinary action registers

Audit teams check whether ledgers and registers are accurately kept. They also ensure that procedures are followed when they verify if the branch manager personally checked all customer installment cards every six months.

Table 17 shows a list of the ledgers kept by each branch, regional and divisional office with the exception of the customer installment card, which remains with Shakti's customers. All ledgers are in the process of being computerized. Once this is completed, auditors will be able to run plausibility checks and benchmark evaluations, which will increase audit's effectiveness and decrease its cost.

Table 17. Ledgers Used to Control Field Operations

Ledger Name	Ledger Function
Ledgers for Branch Offices	
Cash-in-hand Ledger	registers cash at branch office before being deposited at local bank
Cash receipt Ledger	registers installments paid by customers
Transaction book	registers sales of products
Bank Ledger	registers bank account transactions
Customer Ledger	registers transactions with customers
Customer Installment Card	registers payment of installments
Ledgers for Branch, Regional, and Divisional Offices	
Stock ledger	registers stored and delivered equipment
Old equipment ledger	registers unused equipment
Fixed Asset Register	registers office equipment
Personal File	registers staff personal data
Disciplinary Register	registers staff misbehavior
Movement Register	registers staff travel: destination, reason, time of departure and arrival

A Market for New Ideas

Shakti views the audit as an internal market for new ideas. Audit teams are always thinking ahead, always searching for new ways to upgrade services and lower costs. Often they anticipate problems and suggest solutions before the problems become serious, for example when Shakti was spending 600,000 Taka per month for transporting solar systems to its customers.

For almost a decade, management had considered solar system delivery a necessary service, until audit pointed out the time and money this cost the company and suggested alternatives. As a result, management had to reconsider its policy. Branches were instructed to explain to their customers that because Shakti was installing thousands of solar home systems per month, it could no longer bear the transport costs, but would continue to guarantee 100 percent quality maintenance for three years. "We left it up to the branch managers when to begin with the new policy," explains a senior manager. "They know their customers best. But what surprised all of us is how readily customers arranged for the transport of their solar systems. What they cared about most was guaranteed maintenance."

Fund management is another instance where audit contributed valuable suggestions. "We were talking to the manager of a large branch", an audit team reported, "and learned that money would lie idle in the local bank for a month before being transferred to the Shakti account in Dhaka, where it can earn more interest. The branch had around 400 customers and was depositing up to 21,000 Taka a day at the local bank. By the end of the month over 300,000 Taka had accumulated in the branch's account—money which the company needed in Dhaka." Shakti was losing money, at this local bank and in many others as well.

Audit proposed a solution to the problem, providing the branch office had an account at a local Grameen Bank branch: a standing order instructed all money to be transferred to the main Shakti account in Dhaka if the local account exceeded 20,000 Taka. This policy continues to this day.

Internal auditors are concerned with every aspect of the company's business: staff concerns and discipline, logistics and cost effectiveness, account accuracy and fund management. The following episode illustrates a more sensitive aspect: dealing with problem customers. Audit teams enjoy respect in rural communities and are sometimes needed to motivate landlords, politicians, and other people with influence who are disinclined to pay their installments.

When talking to customers, audit teams must be as skilled as they are polite in order to get to the root of a problem. In most cases they can convince the customers to resume payment for their solar systems; the most difficult cases occur when customers are ill mannered. But there are times when audit teams are surprised to hear that it is the customer who has a complaint. They learn that the branch staff member didn't come at the appointed time; that he was short-tempered or even became cross. In such cases, audit teams listen carefully and then encourage an open discussion with the customer and branch staff. When all the facts are in, audit teams negotiate a solution to the problem, and Grameen Shakti maintains its good reputation.

"Internal auditors never assume to know the answers, which is why they are always asking questions," observes a divisional manager. "While discussing marketing techniques following the audit at one of my branches, the audit team first listened to branch staff's complaints about losing customers because they had no more 50W panels in stock. The auditors responded by asking what size panels they did have on hand, and what their strategy to keep their customers might be. Then they let branch staff come up with a few good answers before helping them with suggestions. A lively discussion followed, since audit teams experience what works at many different branches and could give good feedback. But it was their *questions*, which motivated the staff members to look at the problem differently. Instead of making a complaint, they had to think of a solution."

Audit teams ask pointed questions because they have a good idea where problems may arise. When they ask branch staff how many paid-up solar customers have signed contracts for post-warranty maintenance, they do so because they know this is a weak spot at many branches. Auditors understand that branch engineers prefer winning new customers and achieving their quotas. But they also remind them that Shakti stands for service—for the life of the solar system.

Keeping the Balance

By December 2010, Shakti had eighty-four certified accountants auditing its fourteen divisions every six months. Decentralizing audit to the divisions had increased company efficiency, since travel from Dhaka was no longer necessary. Divisional offices are always located in towns or district capitals, which is another reason the transition went smoothly. Accountants could work closer to home and enjoy the conveniences of a town, while not having to bear the high living expenses in Dhaka. Each divisional audit department has six accountants working in the same building as the divisional manager, but they are not under his authority. Audit teams report directly to the managing director.

Auditors work in groups of two, whereby one team member is always more experienced than his colleague. When visiting a branch, however, the less experienced accountant does the talking. "We know that people learn faster in groups of two," an audit coordinator explains. "But we make certain experienced auditors are always on hand to train them. We also rotate accountants to other divisions from time to time—another good proposal from audit to bring fresh ideas into the company."

One example is the solution found for the hundreds of defective solar panels that were accumulating at branch offices. The panels couldn't be resold, and storage was becoming a serious problem. Audit teams wanted to know if they couldn't be repaired and took up the matter with the technology department at the head office. Combined action by s audit teams, engineers, and battery specialists generated valuable synergetic effects that the company then used to benefit its customers. Shakti launched a new project to set up battery charging stations with repaired solar panels at each of its branches and made the service free of charge for all its customers.

In 2010, audit teams faced challenges generated by expansion more than ever. A thousand branches, regional, and divisional offices needed auditing. Branches handled around 700,000 Taka a month, which had to be monitored. Travel costs had skyrocketed, requiring close examination of a branch's movement register. Audit teams still visited customers who were defaulting on payments, but an average division now had 40,000 customers. How do they manage?

An audit team describes its work at a typical branch: "An average branch has around 1,000 solar customers. We can cover about 100 customers while at the branch and know which customers to visit first. We usually begin with new customers and check their installment cards. This is a good indicator of how the branch is working. We like to visit customers defaulting on install-ments during the harvest season to remind them. Then they can't say they are short on funds. We spend up to ten days at a branch and return every six months. If we think there is a problem, we return unannounced for a *quick audit* within a few days. We have a good idea of what can go wrong and how to remedy mistakes. But most of all, we understand people. It's all a matter of experience."

And yet, companies in the industrialized world will wonder why, in a large organization like Shakti, auditing works at all without computerization. "We need more than computers to run a good company," the head of admin-istration and author of the audit guidelines explains. "The overall purpose of the internal audit is to create a reliable and responsible staff. It brings out the best in young people when they become responsible for Shakti's success. I see this so often. We like to think of audit as the eyes of management. But if you have over 8,000 responsible employees there are thousands of eyes watching over the organization. Branch and regional managers are often the ones who spot mistakes and inform audit. This is transparency. Audit holds our compa-ny in balance."

Preparing for Tomorrow's Challenges

> *To succeed as entrepreneur and innovator,*
> *a company has to create a structure which*
> *allows people to be entrepreneurial.*
> —Peter Drucker

If Bangladesh were a developed country and its villages well organized; if experienced personnel were readily available in remote areas; and if, at last, all employees had computers linked by broadband, then Grameen Shakti would have evolved differently. Companies abroad employ central sales departments, outsource branch operations to franchises, and use computer networks to tie their operations together. As a rural company, Shakti couldn't develop in this way. And yet the organization is still effective.

Its managers travel the country and meet frequently—and this is vital to rural business. It is how Shakti manages operations in remote areas like Dhobaura, the Chittagong Hill Tracts, and Ashtamir Char. "If I had to describe Shakti's forte," comments a senior manager, "I would say it's our ability to network and keep in touch. Over the years, our unique way of networking has become a great asset. And the more we grow and decentralize in future, the more we will rely on our network of personal contacts and relations."

This network is still evolving. In the early years, everyone in the company knew everyone else. The pioneering engineers often had worked and roughed it together; they had trained each other, relied on each other, and shared the same problems. Shakti felt like a big family. The entire team met regularly in Dhaka. As a newcomer to solar system technology and its market, the organization had to pool the experiences of every single employee. They had to communicate well to perform well. This is why all branch and head office managers took the time to meet, to get to know one another, and to listen to each other.

Shakti kept this network of communication in place as it grew. Head office managers met regularly with branch staff; regional managers' meetings were held every month in Dhaka. Shakti also let its field staff rotate. This meant changing tasks and locations as well as working with new colleagues every few years. A tightly knit network emerged.

By 2007 Shakti had evolved into a decentralized company with a strong audit and a focus on service. Its first decade of development defined its inner workings, its goals and principles, and its unique company structure. Many cultural aspects of its management are rooted in Bangladeshi customs and its Grameen background, and remain, by nature, ill defined.

The organization's formal structure, on the other hand, is clearly defined. Its geographical breakdown in zones, divisions, regions, and branches reflects a rural service company (see figure 9) But it fails to show the subtle company network. Nor does the formal control structure say anything about the company's informal decision-making processes. The challenge Shakti now faces after a decade of growth is to optimize a highly decentralized organization while preserving its traditional practice of consensus and joint decision making.

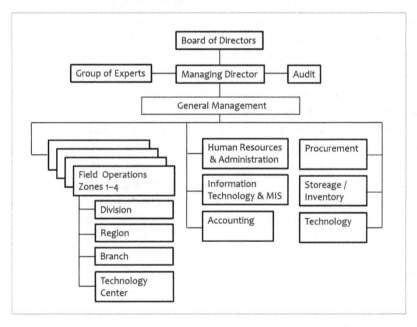

Organogram of Grameen Shakti

Managing Via Joint Decisions in an Open Forum

Shakti managers like to work in teams, be where the action is, and want to be involved in the company as a whole. The meetings during which field and head office managers met in Dhaka were from the beginning an open forum for discussion and decisions for this very reason. Here, branch managers had a chance to voice their opinions and confer about plans. They reported their successes, but also discussed their problems with travel, communication, and lack of staff. It was because of meetings like these that branch managers were provided with mobile phones and motorcycles. Head office managers in Dhaka heard exactly what was happening out in the field and learned where action was needed most.

Like nothing else, the managers' forums shaped the company's culture and laid the groundwork for growth. When branch managers became too numerous to meet at the head office, preparatory meetings were held on a regional and divisional scale. This kept Shakti's network intact, since each branch was reviewed prior to the monthly managers' meeting in Dhaka where regional and divisional managers met with their colleagues at the head office.

Managers' meetings cover all important issues: branch, regional and divisional progress, accounts, audits, procurement, production and technical issues, customer service and marketing, salaries and benefits, staff ideas and customer suggestions, quotas, and future expansion. A few—often new—branch managers were invited to participate to get the big picture of the company and its decision making process. They were encouraged to ask questions and share their ideas.

Managers' meetings to this day are highly interactive. Everyone participates. Most field managers have traveled a full day just to attend the meeting—by rickshaw, boat, steamer, and bus. They're glad to see their colleagues, hear what they have to say, and share how business is developing in their divisions. Bangladeshis are naturally curious and eager to discuss. It's part of their culture. Managers' meetings, therefore, provide an ideal platform to exchange experiences.

"Take for instance the sessions when we review quotas and recovery rates for a branch," comments a head office manager. "Let's say, its monthly quota in 2007 was for 40 solar systems, yet this particular branch installed 50 systems. 'Good work, we would say.' We would also ask why another branch had such a low installment collection rate. New staff was the answer. What's to be done? Regional managers reported similar problems with their branches and offered advice. Head office managers asked if any help was needed with problem customers. A lively discussion was certain to follow, since all managers shared the common goal that branches achieve 100 percent recovery."

Quotas were always a hot topic of discussion, because they were set for individual branch employees. Regional managers first met with their branches and divisional managers to determine their monthly quotas. They came to Dhaka prepared with their proposals and hashed out details with the head office. Typical questions were "Your quota for next month is only slightly higher than the last month. Can you do better?" "Not right now, our new branches can handle only six customers each," was a typical reply. The discussion also gave field managers a chance to share their success. If a divisional manager reported his division achieved its monthly quota 100 percent, his colleagues applauded.

At the end of each manager's meeting, monthly quotas were agreed upon, then printed, distributed, and signed. Field managers knew exactly what they had agreed to accomplish in the following month and felt responsible for doing their part. Everyone knew the company was on schedule and on its way to installing a million solar systems.

"When we set this target a few years ago, many of us thought it would be amazing if we could achieve this in rural Bangladesh," recalls a divisional manager. "But even more incredible is the dynamic such a decision creates in the company. Everybody owns it because the decision was reached by consensus. Not by decree from the head office."

Shifting Control to the Field

By 2008, nearly a hundred head office and field managers were sitting in triple rows around the conference table in Dhaka. The number of regional and divisional managers had doubled to eighty in only one year as a result of expansion. Monthly managers' meetings had become too large and too expensive to be effective. They had to be reorganized.

Divisional managers proposed how this could be done: They would still meet at the head office and invite a few of their regional managers to accompany them. They could rotate the roster each month to get different perspectives from the field and give every regional manager a chance to attend at some point. Monthly regional managers' meetings with the branches in each division plus frequent visits to the field would still be the basis for determining quotas and keep the communication network intact. This would help the company move forward and expand. And it did.

When only two years later Shakti had more than one thousand field offices, regular meetings in the field and at the head office helped keep managers aligned on important decisions. An example is the managers' discussion on the issue of salaries and reducing costs. When the head of accounting talked about the upcoming raise of the pay scale, he was asking divisional managers a few months in advance how the company should handle what staff members were asking: a substantial raise in salary for 9,000 employees,

99 percent of whom were working in field offices. He was not disagreeing, but asking what impact it would have on the company.

"Will Shakti lose money," the manager of accounts asked. "Improved cooking stoves are not yet profitable because we want to improve rural health conditions as fast as possible. Should Shakti raise the price of the stoves? Or of solar home systems?" This would have to be discussed at the branch, regional, and divisional levels. Shakti was no longer a small company with a few hundred employees. Field and head office managers had to prepare their response months in advance of such major decisions.

Specialized branches for improved cooking stoves should increase sales and thus help solve the problem. The reason was simple: branch staff prefers selling solar systems over cooking stoves; specialized branches would market only stoves. Two hundred stove branches with specially trained technicians were installed in 2010 to help solve the problem. But branch staff still lacked experience, and their branches were not sustainable. Shakti was losing money.

"Are we doing enough?" head office improved stove experts asked divisional managers. "To break even, specialized branches should be doing 200 installations per month, but most are installing only 140 stoves. How can we support them?" Not unlike the early days, divisional managers, many of whom had pioneered Shakti's first branches, shared ideas on how they could optimize branch operations. Certainly these branches should get increased support, was the general consensus. There were several examples of sustainable stove branches on the table to show how this could be achieved. But the managers contended that the long-term solution was to address the problem at its root, by shifting more control from the head office to the field.

In order to strengthen the field organization, all branches will in future gain more control. They will operate as profit centers and be responsible for their costs, revenues, and profits. This will add to Shakti's expertise, since more decision-making authority will provide branch managers with a broader spectrum of experience and prepare them for higher-level positions. With few exceptions, all of Shakti's regional, divisional, and zonal managers began their careers at the branch.

Added responsibility and the authority that goes with it provides incentives for field managers to put out their best efforts. But decentralizing control works well only if a thousand field offices stay in sync with the organization's goals and strategies. A system of checks and balances is needed.

Audit teams therefore conduct branch performance evaluations to motivate managers to make decisions that are in the best interests of the company. Regional and divisional managers keep in close contact with their branches, analyse problems, spot opportunities, and give advice. Head office managers make regular field visits for hiring, training, and monitoring equipment; zonal managers visit each of their divisions a few days every month. Together they communicate company goals and streamline Shakti's reporting system.

Newly introduced field visit reports, for example, document regional managers' visits to their branches. "We needed a checklist to follow up on matters discussed maybe six months earlier," explains a zonal manager. "Checklists don't replace the personal attention regional managers give their branches, but are a good way to remind them 'we talked about this a few months ago, is it still a problem? How did you solve it?'"

The ability to solve problems is so essential to rural business, that it factors into an employee's Annual Confidentiality Report, used when he or she is up for promotion and when the contracts are renewed. "All employees' contracts must be renewed every three years, so nothing can be taken for granted," adds the zonal manager "If a branch manager is doing good work, he or she has nothing to worry about. This also applies to me. Every Shakti employee receives a confidentiality report from his or her immediate supervisor. In a tough business like ours, this helps keep everyone alert and proactive."

Technology to Optimize a Decentralized Company

During its first ten years, written reports and meetings were the means to monitor Shakti's operations. By 2005, managers began sharing information via mobile phone on a daily basis: all branch, regional, and divisional offices reported their latest information about product installations to the head office through text messaging. Here, the daily sales information for each product group was compiled and disseminated via SMS by 10 o'clock every morning. The information was also part of a database which could be browsed via cell phone. Managers knew immediately what progress had been made.

Mobile phones fundamentally changed and improved Shakti's business. All branch offices were equipped with mobile phones, and their numbers were published in the company's brochures and product information leaflets. Head office and field managers used their cell phones as a mobile office during their long trips to field offices. They received the latest information from their colleagues and had time to discuss the situation while on the road. In the absence of a computer network, cell phone calls and text messaging allowed information to flow quickly and effectively on all company levels.

By 2010, all fourteen divisional offices used the Internet to forward daily sales information to the head office per e-mail. Gone were the days when divisional managers delivered this information on compact discs. Daily sales information will soon be available on Shakti's intranet; information on inventory, customers, and accounting will be accessible online. As the company continues to expand operations, accounting, procurement, planning, and auditing will benefit significantly from timely data. Computerized information management, often taken for granted in industrialized countries, is finally arriving in Shakti's corner of the world.

No doubt, computerization is long overdue in a highly decentralized organization like Shakti. But if managers' meetings were the company's prime means of compensating for the lack of computers, why then have they not diminished in importance when field offices are networked and online? Open discussion among Shakti's managers has in fact gained in importance as the company grows and decentralizes.

A Problem Solved in Time

When viewed as a system, Shakti's network of managers provides self-correcting mechanisms. Of course, managers compete with one another. But they also jointly tackle problems when they meet. When managers discuss problems openly and fact the facts, they get a sense of what is going wrong in time to act upon it. Excerpts from discussions in a divisional managers' meeting at the head office in 2010 show what this means in practice.

"Almost half of my branch managers have only two months experience; 30 percent of my field staff are dropping out or being hired away. Okay, I know this is nothing new in my division. It's always been a problem to recruit staff in Syhlet, especially in the low-lying *Haor* region, where staff has to travel by boat most of the year. But I still have to keep these branches staffed. They make up one third of my division. Hiring is not the main problem. Over 100 people answered to our newspaper job ads. The problem is getting them to stay on once they've been trained. Field assistants are being hired away by our competitors to become managers for double their salaries."

"You're right; working in the *Haor* is tough. But what makes our company so different is that we go deep into the rural areas our

competitors avoid. My biggest problem in the Hill Tracts is the conflict between tribal people in the hills and the people in the plains.
Extremists even threatened to burn down our offices. We stayed on.
We now have 61 branches installing 1,000 solar systems and as many
improved cooking stoves per month for a grateful clientele. But I
badly need more staff."

"I have over 700 skilled staff working on the delta. Patharghata,
the area hardest hit by Cyclone Sidr three years ago, is now my division's most successful region because of its excellent staff. Business
is good. I plan to hire over 300 new field staff in 2011. What we need
is more management training to keep up with expansion. Shakti can
only excel with a high caliber staff. There is no alternative."

As a result of discussions like these, Shakti established a management
training institute in Dhaka and is planning to open a training center in Comilla. It was decided that in future all divisions will help recruit staff for Sylhet.
An upcoming raise of the pay scale should help attract engineers and curb
poaching field staff.

"When you think about it, all rural companies deal with a shortage of
qualified staff," notes a zonal manager. "But I am optimistic. We excel in
training, and have a strong communication network in place. We all know
our work is making a difference in the lives of the village people. The longer
we are with Shakti, the more we own it. I am sure we'll manage growth."

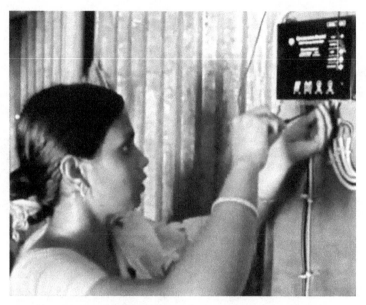

Energy entrepreneur at work

Energy entrepreneur at work

6

Working at the Cutting Edge of Business

The legendary sage of business management, Peter Drucker, claimed you can't do healthy business in a sick society. He might have had business in poor rural societies in mind. Shakti's business lives in underdeveloped rural communities. It is limited to those who can afford a solar system or biogas plant. There are millions more who can't. Shakti's easy credit terms have changed things for the better, but the challenge remains: How to do business with the many poor? How to work at the cutting edge of rural business?

There is no simple answer to these questions, no easy solution, no silver bullet. Shakti takes many approaches to advance its business: it experiments, succeeds, and fails. It strives to keep prices low, streamlines the organization, and exploits technological advancement. But Shakti knows that in the long run, its business is determined by village society; the healthier the rural community, the better the business, the more people benefit.

No one can work miracles in a traditional rural society, but entrepreneurship, new jobs, and social innovation can make a difference. The following illustrates what this means in practice, and why Shakti's overall goal is to advance village communities—the true north for the course of the company.

Entrepreneurs Become a Hallmark of Shakti

A Micro-utility Serving a Clientele of Three

Sharing expensive technology can serve many users, even poor users. More than a decade ago, Grameen Bank led the way with its village phone innovation: a Grameen borrower received a loan to buy a mobile phone and let other villagers use the phone for a small fee. Though the principle of sharing is well known in many developing countries, its practical implementation can be demanding. It needs an entrepreneur to take the initiative and risk, and a partner with funds and know-how.

Mr. Gazi is one of thousands of entrepreneurs who owns a solar system. Typical for rural Bangladesh, he runs a small shop at a village market and earns a modest monthly income of about 5,000 Taka. Not typical is that he can afford a 50W solar system for five times more than what he earns in a month.

He can afford the solar system because he earns money using it. In addition to selling groceries at the market, he is a small-scale energy service provider, a micro-utility, serving a clientele of three. His solar system powers four lamps, but he uses only one to light his shop. He rents the other three lamps to his neighbors, shop owners like himself. All four benefit from solar electricity: Mr. Gazi from the monthly rental fees and Shakti's easy credit terms.

Shakti's financial model for micro-utilities is simple and adaptable. Micro-utility entrepreneurs need pay only 10 percent down, pay no service charge, and enjoy an extended repayment period of three and a half years. In the case of Mr. Gazi, a branch engineer first calculated if the shop owner could make a profit after paying his monthly installment. Shakti then provided one lamp for half price to help get him started. He paid full price for the remaining three lamps and backed the expense by renting them to neighboring shop owners. Branch staff provided training and maintenance free of cost and were close at hand when Mr. Gazi had problems. Today, he has repaid his loan, owns the solar system, and enjoys additional income.

Table 18 lists micro-utility entrepreneurs, who were among the first to risk taking a micro-utility loan for their solar systems in 2004. The table also shows how the shopkeepers turned a profit, since their monthly income from renting out lamps exceeds the amount of their monthly installments.

Table 18. Characteristics of micro-utilities

SHS Owner	SHS	Devices Used by Owner	No. Lamps Rented Out	Rent per Lamp & Day (Taka)	Monthly Installment for SHS (Taka)	Monthly Rent/ Income (Taka)
Gazi	50W 4 lamps	1 lamp 1 TV	3	6	482.14	540
Ali	60W 5 lamps	2 lamps 1 TV	3	6	525.00	540
Hossain	65W 6 lamps	2 lamps	4	6	620.00	720

Shakti provides training, financing, and technology to more than 10,000 micro-utility entrepreneurs. Everyone benefits. Shakti reaches low-income villagers like Mr. Gazi, who otherwise could not afford a solar system. And the company learns about a new sector of the market from its clever customers.

Two brothers in a remote off-grid market in Sylhet, for example, became joint owners of a 50W solar system with four lamps, one TV, and a mobile charger. The grocery shop owner uses one of the lamps in his shop and a second in his storeroom; his brother enjoys the third lamp in addition to electricity for the TV in his pharmacy; and the fourth lamp is rented to a neighboring tea stall for 300 Taka a month. As joint micro-utility owners, the two brothers pay low monthly installments (389 Taka each), earn from lamp rental (150 Taka each), and save more than 500 Taka each on kerosene.

Table 19. Jointly Owned SHS: Expenditures and Savings per Party (Taka)

Monthly Installment for SHS	Monthly Rent/Income from Lamp	Monthly Expenditure for SHS (Installment minus rent)	Monthly Expenditure for Kerosene (without SHS)		Future Monthly Savings
			2005	2007	
389	150	239	450	630	1,080

Making solar systems affordable to low-income customers is only half the battle, however. Learning what convinces customers to invest their sparse resources in expensive technology is the other job of the social engineer: "I learned the most just by listening," explains the branch manager "There was a lot of competition in markets nearby, so lighting for shops after dark plus saving money on kerosene was the best argument for solar electricity. Television attracts customers because it is still rare in off-grid villages, so shopkeepers liked this idea. And the solar lamp may well save all three shops from burning to the ground. The only light in the grocery storeroom came from a kerosene lamp located directly over huge barrels of diesel. My customers completely underestimated the danger of fire. What they feared most was the risk of a micro-utility business. What if it fails and they're stuck with paying off an expensive solar system?"

A Partnership to Share Risk

If, for example, a shop owner who can just manage to support his family buys an expensive solar home system, his family's well-being depends on it. He must make certain it is not stolen or damaged. He has to learn all he can about maintaining it, because he knows his clients will pay only if their solar lamps keep burning. His lamp rental service must function, today and for years to come.

Micro-utilities work because Shakti shoulders some of the risk. It keeps the system operational, trains its owner free of cost, and helps customers avoid repayment problems. If necessary, Shakti takes the solar system back.

Thousands of micro-utilities are now in operation, run by shopkeepers, private households, and cattle and poultry farmers. The micro-utility model therefore varies. Low-income solar micro-utility owners like Mr. Gazi enjoy relaxed loan conditions to reduce their financial burden; the two brothers could afford to pay for their solar system in three years with a 6 % service charge. Biogas micro-utilitieswill be discussed in the next section.

When adapting the micro-utility model to different customers, Shakti often has to improvise with very low margins. And still, Shakti benefits— often in unspectacular ways. 10,000 solar micro-utilities for a poor clientele may not seem like much. But this also means 30,000 well-lit shops in crowded bazaars and a splendid demonstration of solar-powered light. Most of all, micro-utility entrepreneurs signify Shakti's determination to succeed in a low-margin sector of the market to help rural communities thrive.

Biogas Entrepreneurs

In spite of Bangladesh's ample supply of natural gas, biogas has great potential in rural areas. It need not be brought up from hundreds of feet below ground, be liquefied, or be piped and distributed though large networks.

Biomass and water are readily available in rural Bangladesh. Biogas, like solar energy, can be produced where needed.

In 2005, Shakti launched the pilot phase of its biogas program for small farms and private households. It hired civil engineers, trained masons, developed training programs, and constructed 450 biogas plants. Shakti's branches were challenged with creating a market for a new and expensive technology. And what better way to raise the interest of potential biogas customers than with the prospects of earning money as owners of a micro-utility.

Farmers like Mr. Razzaque, for example, who owned more than a thousand chickens. His farm was ideally located near several houses and a local market with restaurants and tea stalls—all perfect conditions for a biogas micro-utility, which a good businessman like Razzaque was quick to understand. His 9 m³ plant produces enough biogas to feed several cooking stoves and to power a mantle lamp and a 2 kW gas-powered generator. As a micro-utility entrepreneur, he has a clientele of thirteen, each of whom pays him 400 Taka a month for a biogas line to his plant.

"When introducing a new product, we need customers like Mr. Razzaque to demonstrate its benefits," an experienced branch engineer explains. "Let people see the technology, touch it, talk about it at the market. Let them discuss with biogas pioneers and hear firsthand from customers like Mr. Maola, why he has invested in his third biogas plant."

Maola raises 3,000 chickens on his farm near the Dhaka airport. When you talk to him, you sense at once that he is an entrepreneur with heart and soul. He quickly recognized the market opportunity of a biogas micro-utility near Dhaka. Liquefied petroleum gas (LPG) cost him 1,800 Taka a month in addition to the 1,000 Taka he was paying for firewood. A biogas plant could also be put to good use for what usually just cost him money to remove: the huge amount of dung produced by his 3,000 chickens.

Maola first invested in a 6 m³ plant and easily found biogas customers in the densely populated area outside Dhaka. Everything worked out better than expected, and soon more neighbors wanted biogas than he could accommodate. He invested in a second 6 m³ plant and later in a third (4.8 m³). His plants now supply twenty-three families with biogas, generating an income of 8,050 Taka per month. He has full ownership of two biogas plants and will finance the third in less than two years with a loan from Shakti.

Like thousands of other micro-utility owners, Razzaque and Maola are local entrepreneurs. Their biogas plants digest local resources. The gas produced sells locally, which helps both the entrepreneurs and their village customers save on wood and imported kerosene. Local technicians and masons earn money by building and maintaining the biogas plants. Their money stays in the village and this helps villages thrive.

The success of Shakti's first biogas micro-utilities inspired business ideas in others. Ms. Hazera, provides an example. She lives with her family of five in a village in Sonargaon County, about 20 kilometers from Dhaka. She has no farm, no cows, and no chickens or ducks, but she is the owner of a 6 m³ biogas plant with nine gas lines to nearby houses. How does this work? She collects the dung for her plant from the chickens and cows of her neighbors, who are more than happy to get rid of the smelly waste. Her customers also welcome saving money on clean cooking fuel, since liquefied petroleum gas is steadily increasing in price.

Today, Hazera is an experienced micro-utility entrepreneur. She has paid off her biogas plant and offers her customers a continuous supply of clean energy at a competitive price of 350 Taka per month. As Hazera sees it, "The main thing is to keep my customers happy and to stay in business." And she does.

But what company would support such a bizarre business idea? Put itself at risk by giving Hazera a loan for a 6 m³ biogas plant? And then go to the expense of installing nine gas lines to nearby houses? It's amazing that Shakti engineers even listened to her. If she makes the price competitive, she doesn't earn a big profit. But she must still pay back her loan and have enough money left to support her four children.

Hazera's business depends on Shakti's micro-utility model, which is fine-tuned to small scale entrepreneurs. Financing is exactly tailored to Hazera's business needs. She can handle the technology because it is not too complicated. Shakti engineers back her up with all services she needs: installing gas lines, training, maintenance, and repair. It's the clever combination of all these components that gives Shakti its edge.

An Academic Enters the Fertilizer Business

Mr. Khaledur has a master's degree in Bangla and left his city job to become a cattle farmer. He owns land in a rural area in Chittagong and employs eight farm workers and one cook. While negotiating the sale of a biogas plant, a branch engineer discussed how the young farmer could get a return on his investment of 35,000 Taka. His 4.8 m³ plant produced enough biogas to fuel three cook stoves, but he needed only two: one for cooking meals for his nine employees, and a second for cooking the 60 kg of rice husks, straw, and vegetables needed to nourish his bullocks.

Khaledur showed little interest in a biogas micro-utility, since neighboring houses were too far away. What piqued the cattle farmer's curiosity was how he could become a supplier of organic fertilizer. The branch engineer calculated his biogas plant could yield as much as 20,000 Taka worth of bio slurry per year, a promising business for a farmer who was fattening thirty cows for the upcoming Eid festival.

As a farmer, Khaledur understood the benefits of bio slurry for his land. But as a businessman, he recognized a growing market for fertilizer that is not imported, which is key to Shakti's marketing strategy for Jaibo Shar. Shakti counts on entrepreneurial farmers like Khaledur to market its organic fertilizer. If marketed successfully, farmers profit from increased crop yield and an abundant supply of bio slurry at local markets, and biogas owners benefit from a new source of income. The fertilizer business further adds to the village economy, because the production, collection, and refinement of bio slurry create local jobs.

Whatever the product Shakti introduces, generating income for villagers is part of the package to spur economic growth. Since introducing solar home systems in 1996, Shakti has trained and employed thousands of solar technicians and field assistants. Shakti's biogas program increased incomes for micro-utility entrepreneurs and created jobs for local masons. In the crisis area Kurigram, where jobs and skilled workers are particularly scarce, Shakti is training women as assistant masons. "Women in Bangladesh can do this," claims the engineer in charge of training. "We're optimistic they will later become full-fledged masons and earn as entrepreneurs."

Cooking Stove Entrepreneurs

When in 2007 a regional manager in Phulpur envisioned the first improved-cooking-stove-town with 400 stoves in use, his colleagues praised his optimism and wished him luck. Only three years later, Phulpur Town had 600 cooks preparing food on improved stoves in restaurants, schools, and private households. . Even more surprising was that Phulpur, Shakti's pioneering solar community, was installing more improved cooking stoves per month than solar home systems. What caused the breakthrough?

First of all: failure. More precisely, going from one failure to another with no loss of enthusiasm, which is how Winston Churchill defined success. Everything went well at the start. During the first year of the program, Shakti trained and certified 625 local stove technicians. Branch staff took part in the trainers' programs to provide expertise at the branch level; stove trainers were installed in each of Shakti's sixty regional offices for supervision. Field staff also supported locals to make a success of their business as stove entrepreneurs, because most of them were from poor families and with little schooling.

And, indeed, there were some very talented artisans. Villagers like Arif, a twenty-two-year-old stove technician in Phulpur, for example. Arif quickly mastered the art of constructing a flawless stove and soon was earning 6,000 Taka a month. Or young Muhammad in Sylhet, who despite a physical handicap with his left arm, became an excellent technician. And yet, fewer than 50 percent of the trainees were skilled enough to construct a flawless stove.

"Inexact measurements were the main problem," explained Shakti's chief coordinator of the training program. "Then smoke and fire escaped from the mouth and the chimney; or the cast iron grate for the firewood fell through to the ground. Mixing the clay was also a problem for the local technicians, since it sometimes had to be mixed with straw, cow dung, and jute or rice husks to make it more durable. Often, it fractures."

Nevertheless, 30,000 stoves were successfully installed during the first four years of the improved stove program, many of them on the delta, where Cyclone Sidr had caused extensive tree-damage and made firewood scarce. This success was due mainly to Shakti's painstaking supervision. But it couldn't change the deficiencies of the mud stove model itself. Nor could it make up for the skills needed by village entrepreneurs to construct flawless stoves.

The problems escalated as Shakti expanded; during the six-month warranty period, the company was responsible for all repairs and had to replace the stove if it was defect. Shakti went back to the drawing board and came up with a stove made of concrete. It could be prefabricated, mass produced, and quickly and easily installed—even by village women. A branch manager explains how business with the new stove created new opportunities for village entrepreneurs.

"First we encourage women to apply for a job as a stove technician. If accepted, they receive training and a tool-set, and start working for a basic monthly salary of 3,000 Taka as Shakti certified technicians. Their starting salary is low to encourage them to become part-time entrepreneurs who find and serve new customers on their own. They receive 50 Taka for each of the first ten cooking stoves they install per month, but 150 Taka for every additional stove. That's around 5,000 Taka a month for only twenty new customers. This is the heart of Shakti's new marketing strategy. Women earn more if working on their own. Shakti's role is to help women technicians get started as stove entrepreneurs."

The branch in Noyer in the Comilla division, for example, employs four village women technicians. Ms. Maksuda, the branch's first stove technician, describes a typical working day:

"When I go to a customer's house to install a stove, many village women want to come along and watch. I invite them all. I can do this because I am a woman. The customer has paid for the transport of the heavy concrete stove in advance, so it's waiting for us in the kitchen when we arrive. I adjust the height of the stove and mount the chimney, usually by cutting a hole in the roof. But what I enjoy most is answering everyone's questions. Women laugh when they hear it takes only ten to fifteen minutes to boil water— half the time it takes on a mud stove. Or that we can cook dinner the same evening to celebrate—instead of waiting over a week for the mud stove to dry. It's fun. Some women buy a new stove on the spot."

The Noyer branch specializes in improved cooking stoves. Its full-time staff of four markets neither solar systems nor biogas plants, but works together with its four part-time women entrepreneurs to market and install stoves. Shakti's novel marketing strategy coupled with specialized branches and the new concrete stove model caused a breakthrough in the improved stove market.

By 2010, Phulpur town was one of twenty improved-cooking-stove-towns in Bangladesh, many of them with over 1,000 customers. Its regional manager has since moved to the head office to help coordinate the improved stove training program nationwide. There will be no lack of work for him and his three colleagues. Shakti plans to install half a million improved cooking stoves in 2011.

Working at the Cutting Edge

There are no micro-utilities for improved cooking stoves. Ms. Maksuda works as a part-time entrepreneur. But like the owner of the solar micro-utility, Mr. Gazi, she relies on Shakti's financial and technical knowhow and training to start her business. The success of their business in the long run, however, will lie less in the actual training program than it will in Shakti's effective village network for ongoing support. Trained branch staff is on hand when village entrepreneurs need help.

Ms. Maksuda and Mr. Gazi are more than random examples of small-time village dealers of stoves or electricity. They are early role models of a new class of rural energy entrepreneurs. They require risk on the part of Shakti and an extra effort to cultivate. Were Shakti out for short-term profit, it would hardly cater to them. But Shakti believes there will be many entrepreneurs in future and that in the long term, they will be the ones to grow the market.

Thus what looks like a simple concept for creating rural energy entrepreneurs turns out to be a fine-tuned approach in practice, that reveals prominent features of Shakti's future course: the spirit to create business in unconventional ways, the attitude to treat rural people as entrepreneurs, the intention to do business anywhere, and the deep conviction that everyone must make an income.

A stall like Mr. Gazi's

I tell the young girls: "I'm a woman and learned electronics—why can't you?"

Sowing Green Futures with Technology Centers

In 2005, Shakti launched its boldest project yet. It began decentralizing all production from its central factory in Dhaka to rural communities. In future, all solar system accessories will be manufactured and repaired in village production units near Shakti's branch offices. The production units will also function as training centers for village technicians and thus advance energy entrepreneurship far beyond the micro-utility approach.

Local production will boost Shakti's rural business fundamentally. Above all, it will reduce the time and cost of transportation between Shakti's headquarters and its field offices. To keep the branches stocked, all system components had to be transported from Dhaka to hundreds of branch offices throughout Bangladesh. Transportation problems escalated as Shakti continued to expand operations and still had to guarantee a continuous supply of solar system components to its branches.

Getting There Is Only Half the Battle: The Road to Rangamati

Logistics can make or break rural business in Bangladesh. Two-lane highways are shared by buses, cars, trucks, water buffalo carts, three-wheeled taxis, motorbikes, flatbed rickshaws with straw stacked higher than the drivers, bicycles carrying entire families, tractors laden with bamboo—all competing for space. Traffic jams in Dhaka are ceaseless nightmares, temporarily interrupted only by political strikes, which forbid all transport in the city for days at a time. In a country with more navigable waterways than roads, water transport is unavoidable, making deliveries to villages difficult during the rainy season and impossible during floods.

Branch offices located on islands in the Bay of Bengal face different problems. Steamers travel only a few times a week and often are delayed by storms or by getting stuck on sandbanks and chars during dry months. The main roads in the Chittagong Hill Tracts traverse a politically instable region controlled by frequent army checkpoints. But the biggest problem is just getting there from Dhaka.

For example, when the branch office in Rangamati in the Hill Tracts sends a defective mobile phone charger to Dhaka for repair, it travels a 700-km round trip. Shakti's delivery trucks have to take the Dhaka–Chittagong highway, the busiest in the country and plagued by bumper-to-bumper traffic jams. It can take up to four weeks for a mobile phone charger to be repaired and returned to Rangamati. If, however it is repaired locally, the branch could have a functioning mobile charger returned within days.

"We used to replace a defective mobile phone charger with a new one to ensure prompt customer service," explains the procurement manager. "Village production centers will save us money on new solar products, plus the expense of keeping the branch fully stocked."

Women Run Technology Centers

Moving production and repair of solar products to village centers is a major undertaking in rural Bangladesh. But what makes this project so unique is the unprecedented way in which the centers are organized and managed. Grameen Technology Centers (GTCs), as the village production units are called, are set up and operated by women. Women engineers manage all local production and repair of solar system accessories.

As engineers, they have the technical knowledge to master all of this. What will challenge their ingenuity is running a training center for energy entrepreneurs. The candidates for this training ideally are unemployed village women between the ages of eighteen and thirty with at least eight years of schooling, and who are either widowed or divorced.

"But why women engineers?" Shakti's managers were asked. "Are they more diligent, tolerant and resourceful than men? And isn't it far more expensive to set up and staff village technology centers than to have branch engineers do the training?" If it were only a matter of teaching solar technology, this might work. But more was at stake.

About half of the village population are women, many of whom are school dropouts, unskilled, and unemployed. The majority of the solar home system users are women. A large part of Shakti's future business takes place in a woman's world, and Shakti believes women engineers are ideal role models for young village women.

Management also knows from experience that in conservative rural society, women can meet with other women more easily than men can. When a male engineer comes to collect an installment and the woman of the house is at home alone, she will tell him: "My husband is not here. Please come back when he returns this evening." This is no problem for a woman engineer or technician. She can enter the house, service the solar system, and instruct women users in its maintenance even when no male family member is at home. This is a woman's advantage in a rural service company.

We will later see how women engineers teach housewives the basics of solar technology and how they lead school dropouts through theory and practice to jobs and self-esteem. But getting to this point would take three years of trials to achieve. Shakti's first task was to find women engineers who were willing to take up the challenge of setting up a village technology center.

Learning the Meaning of "Remote" and "Off-grid"

The start of the Grameen technology program in 2005 required an enormous effort on the part of Shakti managers. The few women engineers who did apply for a position came mainly from urban areas and from educated families and had little contact with rural communities. Company policy with male engineers was to simply send them to a village branch office and see how they fared. Working with women, in contrast, required cultural considerations, tact, and discretion. Grameen technology engineers are usually in their twenties and single. It is tradition in Bangladesh for women of this age to live at home until they marry. A job at a village technology center required moving away from the safety of their families and working in an unfamiliar environment.

Shakti therefore made sure women engineers had a comfortable and safe place to live and work. The company often rented a building to house the GTC as well as its regional and branch offices, with an entire floor reserved for the technology center. In Rajshahi Town, Shakti rented the ground floor of a house next to its regional office, whose owner lived on the first floor and had a security guard. The women had a fully furnished office at their disposal, including classrooms equipped with videos, solar accessories, tools, and training materials, in addition to their private living quarters. They enjoyed free rent and a good starting salary of 4,000 Taka per month, which Shakti would double after a six-month trial period to be on par with the salary of a branch engineer.

Generous incentives for women engineers eased their transition to the villages. But incentives couldn't lessen the intensity of the tasks waiting for the women when they arrived. Their first challenge was to find candidates for training. Branch staff supported the GTC engineers by asking customers if they knew of unemployed women with at least eight years of schooling. Shakti's good reputation among the rural people gave the Grameen technology program the boost it needed to get started. But young village women often were too shy to come to the technology center's office. Women engineers then had to go to their villages, which could take hours by boat and on foot.

As one of the first women engineers in Rajshahi described it, "Senior managers at the head office tried to prepare us for rural cross-country travel. But you don't really know what you are in for until you are actually in a small boat traversing the mighty Ganges. All I could think of was what would I do if the boat capsized. I was so relieved to finally reach land and thought we had reached our destination. But no, we simply walked to the next river and took another boat. By the time we finally got to the char, we had crossed three rivers and I had learned what it means to work in remote, off-grid villages. It would take me and my two colleagues three months to find the twelve trainees needed to begin our first training session."

Shakti had a support network in place for women engineers through its field managers and staff. A human resource manager describes his work at the head office:

"I called GTC engineers every day to check if they were having any difficulties, and from what I heard we weren't done yet. We would need about two more years to expand and fully refine the technology training center model, but we already had good reason to believe it would succeed.

"The Grameen technology program attracted young women with a pioneering spirit who wanted to apply their knowledge as engineers. One exceptionally motivated engineer contracted typhoid fever on her second day of working in the Hill Tracts and still wanted to continue her job after recovery. We had a young mother from a conservative family who rented a house near the GTC office and engaged her sister to take care of her baby son while she worked. When she applied for the job, we were sceptical this could work in the villages. But she assured us she could manage her job and family even when far away from Dhaka and her in-laws. And she did."

Technology Centers Evolve Step by Step

Shakti developed its new program slowly to learn from women engineers' experiences in the field. It began by setting up five technology centers in different parts of Bangladesh. Each center was run by a team of three women engineers and located near an established branch office. The women met for the first time at the head office in Dhaka, where they were briefed on their duties and received training for the production and repair of solar equipment.

The head of the technology department notes that "We also give them a compact course in accounting and administration to prepare them for managing a technology center. On the technical side, they learn all about solar, cookstove, and biogas technology; we even give them a refresher course on the basics in electronics, since this was taught in their first year of engineering a few years back. The hard part is preparing them for the villages. A technology center is not a simple construct you merely set up and expect to function by producing solar products. Village people have to accept it; it has to become a part of the community."

When in the villages, the team of women engineers received support from the branches when setting up their training program. But the task of convincing young women and their families that the training was worthwhile was left up to the finesse of the women engineers themselves. As an incentive for poor village women to participate in the program, Shakti provided a travel and food allowance (100 Taka per trainee per day) and supplied all equipment and training free of charge. The fifteen-day training program introduced the trainees to renewable energy technologies and trained them to manufacture four solar home system accessories: lamps, DC–DC converters, charge controllers, and mobile phone chargers. The full program is illustrated in the Appendix.

"Around 10 percent of the trainees are excellent, 40 percent good and the rest fair or in need of additional training," summed up a woman engineer after her first training sessions in the Hill Tracts. "I did my best to explain diodes and transistors, used visual aids, paraphrased and repeated everything—only to learn after an hour that several trainees spoke tribal dialects and hadn't understood a word I had said. And those with no language problem were too shy to ask me questions." The GTC engineer in the crisis area in Chilmari added: "Being from a poor family and learning electronics with an eighth-grade education is like learning a foreign language to these girls. They're scared they can't do this. I tell them I'm a woman and learned electronics— why can't they?"

Women engineers were challenged with a more difficult task than teaching electronics. They had to inspire confidence in village women to see themselves differently. During their first two years of trials, they would experience trainees who were quick learners and showed initiative. But all their trainees were poor, needed to earn, and were confined to traditional life in a village and a limited future. An example of two trainees shows why this is a recurring theme in the lives of poor village women.

Selena and Jesmin had both failed their secondary school examinations. Both were eighteen years of age, born in Chilmari, and came from families with seven children; both were divorced. Typical for poor families in rural Bangladesh, they could barely cover their living expenses. Selena's father was a farmer, Jesmin's father was a mason, and both their mothers were house-wives. Selena and Jasmin had brothers working in garment factories in Dhaka and were planning to join them to help earn extra income for their families. Fortunately, women engineers intervened and encouraged them to participate in the GTC solar technicians' training program.

A Major Step for a Village Girl

Selena and Jesmin were among the first young women to complete the tech-nology training and were eager to earn even before the GTC production cen-ter was up and running. "They offered to work for free, just to make sure they would later have a job," recounted the supervising engineer. "We had told them during training that as certified technicians they could work at home and earn by producing solar system accessories. 'But couldn't we start work-ing here now?' they were asking. 'We have no electricity at home.' We made an exception and let them begin work at the technology center. They were so proud. As Grameen Shakti Certified Technicians, they had a title, an income, and were setting an example for other village women to be a solar technician." A woman engineer at the GTC in Rajshahi explains further:

"Village girls don't usually think about learning technology. They major in arts at school, prefer studying history and English and think they'll fail their secondary school exams if they major in sci-ence. But now I think this could change. One of my students was a girl from a poor family and exceptionally intelligent, with an A+ in math, chemistry and physics. When I congratulated her on her ex-ams, she told me she wanted to be an engineer like me. She was sur-prised to hear, she had the ability to attend a polytechnic engineer-ing institute, even a university."

"Even hearing this from me made her afraid. Going beyond the tenth grade had never entered her mind. She was the first in her family to receive a secondary school diploma. Her father, a security guard, earned a modest salary. How would she afford university? 'There are government scholarships', I said. 'And you are good enough to get one.'"

Going from tenth grade to a university diploma is a huge step a village girl from a poor family. Village girls value higher education, but don't believe it to be within reach. Nor do their families. With the women engineers as role

models, poor women come to believe that they can become skilled technicians, even engineers. But this will take time. Many young women from poor
village families are still reluctant to follow this path.

Poor families in rural Bangladesh are deeply rooted in their cultural and
religious traditions. They arrange their daughters' marriages, often before girls
reach the age of eighteen—the minimum legal age for marriage. If girls don't
finish school, they live at home with their families, marry young, and then go
to live with their husband's families to take care of their in-laws, the household, and the children. With no income, they are economically dependent on
their husbands and must accept their fate if their husbands take a second
wife—or far worse—divorce them in pursuit of the dowry of a new bride.

"What options do poor young women have?" asks a GTC engineer, "Women can't own a shop or sell at the market. They seldom
have skills. They can't even cook, which could bring a decent wage in
urban households. They could easily get jobs as domestics in Dhaka,
but refuse this kind of work. Instead they want a real job and prefer
working in a garment factory.

"I grew up in a family of engineers in Dhaka, and had no idea of
the problems poor women face until I met them here in Rajshahi.
Some go to Dhaka to earn, to escape marriage and poverty. They
dream of freedom and self-sufficiency. But a young girl from a poor
village family is in no position to handle a metropolis the size of
Dhaka with 12 million people. She will share deplorable living quarters in slumlord apartments with many other girls, because landlords
won't rent nice rooms to garment factory workers who earn less
than 2,000 Taka a month. She's on her own, unsafe and far away
from the security of her family."

Scholarships to Study at Grameen Tech

Training at a Grameen Technology Center qualifies a young woman for a job
in her own village. She can do freelance business and still live at home with
her family. Her job adds to the family income and her living expenses are low.

"Poor families actually can't afford idle women, this I have
learned in the villages," explains a woman engineer.

"If the male earners of the family fall ill or cannot find work, a
woman's income provides the family's only food. We are giving
women excellent training at no cost to their families; we help them
get started as energy entrepreneurs. In a way, we are granting these

young women scholarships to study at *Grameen Tech*, the Grameen Technology Center. We teach them the basics in electronics, about diodes, integrated circuits, problems with charge controllers, both in theory and practice; they learn about biogas technology, improved cooking stoves and combustion efficiency, about the environment and health.

When they finish their training, the women receive a diploma, tool bag, note pad and pencil, and money to compensate their food and travel expenses. Shakti managers attend their graduation and personally congratulate them. Photos are taken for the Shakti newsletter. Plans are discussed. The new Grameen Shakti Certified Technicians are ready to go to work—in their villages."

During the first year of operation, Grameen Technology Center engineers trained and certified 150 village women as solar technicians and renewable energy entrepreneurs. By 2010 they would number 3,000.

Villages Turn into Manufacturing Hubs

Five years after launching the technology centers, they had turned into solar manufacturing hubs. All production had been decentralized from the head office to forty-six technology centers. They supplied solar system accessories to one thousand branches throughout rural Bangladesh. Local production was vital to Shakti's business, because by 2010, branches were installing 20,000 solar systems a month. The demanding task of coordinating the logistics also had shifted from the head office to the field—more precisely to the divisional offices.

A divisional manager gives an example: "If all sixty-one branches in my division set their monthly quota for a total of 2,000 systems, the technology centers have to supply them with 3,000 charge controllers and 7,500 lamps. I calculate 1,000 of these charge controllers for replacement and repair; solar home systems normally require from three to five lamps. We also keep the branches supplied with 3,000 extra circuits for immediate replacement in addition to around 500 mobile phone chargers and 200 DC–DC converters a month. All of this is coordinated from my office. The rest is up to the GTC engineers."

The rest? The women engineers manage all production and repair plus the work of the freelance technicians. They keep everything on schedule, do quality control, and prevent breakdowns in the supply chain. They travel, train, and motivate. "My division has 400 energy entrepreneurs working at home in their villages, at the GTC office and in the field doing solar system maintenance," explains a divisional manager. "That the GTC engineers can coordinate all of this is an art. But it actually works."

Thamina in front of her technology center with her teachers, GTC engineers

Training Village Girls for Life

On a busy village road in Homna East, there is a sign nailed to a palm tree outside a tiny house made of corrugated tin. It reads: *Thamina's Technology Center: Here solar home system accessories are assembled and repaired—supported by Grameen Shakti.* The technology center inside consists of a table wedged between a bed, cupboard, and plastic tubs, with a soldering iron, a DC power supply, lead wire, cutting pliers, screwdrivers, printed circuit boards, lampshades, mobile chargers, and charge controllers.

Sitting at the table halfway into the open doorway is Thamina, the technology center's owner and chief technician. She has supplied Shakti with solar system accessories for the past three years and earns on average 5,500 Taka a month. She has no father and uses her earnings to help feed her family and keep her brother in school. But she also has plans for herself. Thamina scored first in the Grameen technology training program. She has since taken two refresher courses, does solar system maintenance in her village, and soon will complete twelve years of schooling with a high school diploma.

Inspired by Thamina's success, young Shioly is only four months on the job as a solar technician and already earning more than her husband. With only a fifth-grade education, women engineers had to make an exception for Shioly, "but she is so poor and was eager to earn and provide for her new born baby. We couldn't refuse."

Akhi, a Cyclone Sidr victim, lives with her husband and two-year-old son in her father-in-law's house. As a solar entrepreneur, she makes 600 charge controllers a month and an income of 6,000 Taka—twice the amount her husband earns as a day-laborer. When their incomes are added together, the couple earns almost as much in a month as a primary school teacher or a Shakti branch engineer.

No doubt, a chance to earn an income is a driving force for poor women to go through the Grameen technology training. If a young woman can earn from 4,000 to 6,000 Taka a month as a freelance technician, and if she lives at home and contributes to her family's income, she is doing well. Moreover, she has at least some say in how the money should be spent. Poor families often need extra money for medical care and the education of their sons. Thamina is planning for her own college education. "Then I can get a good job and still do freelance work for Shakti."

More Than a Job: Entrepreneurs Bring Change to the Village

Shefaly and Sabina didn't do the fifteen-day Grameen technology training. Instead they successfully completed the new GTC training program for improved cooking stoves. On their way to a new customer, both young girls wear a burka and are accompanied by a stove technician from the Shakti branch nearby. The concrete stove is installed in less than two hours, for which each of the women entrepreneurs earn 150 Taka. But what makes this story different is that they work together with Sayma.

Sayma was one of the first in Phulpur to complete the GTC program and graduated at the top of her class. On the morning when Shefaly and Sabina were installing the concrete stove, Sayma was on the tin roof of a village house installing a solar panel. Sayma can do everything from the solar system wiring in the house to climbing a steep roof in a burka to install the panel. Later that afternoon, she will return to her immaculate technology center in her family's house and meet with Shefaly and Sabina.

None of the three young women is wearing a burka now since they are working in Sayma's technology center in their own village. And what a difference this makes. They laugh and talk while soldering semiconductors onto circuit boards and making plans for the future. Sabina and Shefaly both want to study; they dream of personal independence. Sayma seems to be leading the way as a solar entrepreneur.

Sayma earns up to 7,000 Taka a month and deposits 1,000 Taka of her income in her savings account at a local Grameen Bank branch. She is twenty-three years old and divorced, has eight years of schooling and is now a successful freelance technician and pays friends to help her. Although her two friends could not do the GTC training, Sayma is training them to help her produce solar components. "With their help I can make 60 to 70 components a day and pay them with my extra earnings."

Both Shefaly and Sabina have twelve years of schooling and high school diplomas. Sayma has no diploma, but she does have drive, energy, and ideas. A Grameen Shakti Achievement Award for 6,000 Taka hangs framed on the wall in her workshop. Sayma gave some of the prize money to her mother and put the rest in the bank. With her savings she later bought a calf, which she will fatten for the market. Her husband would like to come back, but Sayma is not interested. She wants to extend her business. "Before I had nothing, now I have everything. I want to help my friends to earn; I can train them."

This is a breakthrough Shakti had hoped for. Not all technicians will have Sayma's drive, but they can help each other, work together. Many of them will start out small and grow their business with Shakti's support. In the long term, they may provide the company with the entrepreneurial resources it will need to expand the energy market. "We can't expect that all trained technicians will work as entrepreneurs," notes the technical director. "They get married or move away, where we can no longer support them. But 3,000 village women have been trained to be energy entrepreneurs and thousands more will follow as we expand the technology centers to one hundred by 2015. There will be many more entrepreneurs like Sayma and her friends."

Women engineers no longer have difficulty finding village candidates for training. When young women see others like themselves earning an income and when neighbors say "Oh, I hear your daughter is working in electronics," they believe there is no reason why they, too, can't become energy entrepreneurs. Even villagers' natural curiosity promotes the GTC program. When people take notice of the Shakti signboard in front of a technician's house, they ask the young women, "Where did you learn this? Are you an engineer?"

"We tell them to simply say they were trained and certified by Grameen Shakti engineers and have a sign and a certificate to prove it," says a GTC supervisor. "Most encouraging is that Shakti's customers are bringing the technicians their solar lamps and other accessories for minor repairs. This saves branch staff time. But to the young woman technician, this conveys village respect and recognition of her expertise. And this means just as much to a poor woman as a job and an income."

Women Engineers Pioneer the Energy Future

Nearly 200 Grameen technology engineers are working in rural Bangladesh. Ask any one of them why she studied engineering, and she will tell you she liked math and physics in school and had better chances of getting a job. Ask them why they love their job in the villages, and they will tell you because they can apply their knowledge as an engineer and train poor women. A GTC engineer recalls: "Thamina was in the tenth grade when she did the training. Now she's going to college. Even before our production unit was set up, Thamina went to visit solar customers and asked if they were having any problems with their systems; as a Shakti certified technician she could help. Now she's earning 5,000 Taka a month producing solar system accessories. When I see the change in poor women's lives, I know I'm part of it. This gives my life meaning."

Thamina's teacher was one of the first women engineers to apply for the Grameen technology program and the first mother to convince Shakti managers she could manage both her family and her job as a GTC engineer. "I make it work, because I want to work as an engineer. And I love technology."

Shakti furthers women engineers' technical expertise. GTC engineers visit the head office regularly for training. Senior engineers instruct them in the production and repair of all new products. The most recent challenge for women engineers is learning to repair defect solar panels, which will later be reinstalled in battery recharging stations. "They really enjoy doing this," notes Shakti's technical director. "Women engineers are energized by learning new technologies."

Women engineers are competent in many areas and able to turn with ease from one task to another. They are capable production managers, adept in teaching technology and in motivating young women to become freelance technicians. They have successfully adapted to living and working in the villages. Working mothers arrange their families around their jobs, rent houses, and engage help to look after their children. Married engineers accept seeing their husbands once or twice a month. A zonal manager notes that, "To be sure there are problems when families are too far apart, which we try to avoid. But what is surprising is what many women are willing to put up with to keep an interesting job. Even when applying for the job. One woman engineer traveled 500 km just for an interview."

Roughing It at the Branch

The scene has changed since 2005, when Shakti had only a handful of applications for its village technology centers. Hiring is no longer a problem, and major changes have been made in the training program for women engineers. Not unlike the training for branch managers, GTC trainees now begin their six-month training at a Shakti branch. They install and maintain solar systems; market solar, biogas plants, and improved cooking stoves; collect installments; and do all necessary paperwork. They sometimes rent rooms near the branch, but usually stay at a nearby Grameen Technology Center, where they also work part-time.

Some women engineers love the freedom of the work and would go back to the branch in a minute when their training is completed; others are relieved to finally be working at the technology center and not to be out walking for hours in the hot sun, where there are few tube wells for drinking water and no public toilets. A few women engineers had worked at a Shakti branch before the Grameen technology program was launched, so it was not a completely new idea to train women at the branches. More important for the success of the GTC program is why these women engineers stayed on at the branch for up to four years. "The main thing was the good working environment at the branch," explains a former Shakti branch engineer. "My colleagues were always helpful and very polite when talking to me and their customers."

This is important for GTC engineers, who often work with male branch staff in the same building, serve the same customers, and depend on each other's support. Women engineers say they came to Grameen Shakti because they wanted to work for a respected company that is helping the poor. Equally important is that they work with respectful colleagues. "Shakti is known throughout Bangladesh for its polite staff," continues the woman engineer. "That's the training you get at the branch."

"We must be doing something right, because few women engineers quit their jobs," says the technical director in charge of the Grameen technology centers. "We give the engineers a secure job, a good salary, technical training and support. But when the women engineers start their work in the villages, the program develops its own dynamic."

However Beautiful the Strategy—Look at the Results

Any new idea needs practical demonstration, visible proof that it works. That women should play an important role in the rural energy business was a new idea in 2005—at least in the villages of Bangladesh. Today there is evidence that this was a good idea. Shakti's idea placed women in unusual roles in a conservative rural society, where they succeeded as engineers, production managers, and energy entrepreneurs.

Shakti didn't know if conservative villagers would accept school dropouts, widows, and divorcees as sufficiently qualified to maintain their solar systems. A generation ago, this would have been unthinkable. It is not exactly commonplace today, but it is being done with success. The numbers speak for themselves: forty-six technology centers and 3,000 women technicians trained within five years; 1,000 branches served with a continuous supply of solar accessories.

Far more subtle is how the technology centers have become part of village life through their school programs and training for solar system users. While branch staff organizes user training sessions at its office, a mosque, or local market, GTC engineers hold meetings for women users in their technology centers, at schools, or in women's homes in remote areas like a char. And from the start, women engineers reported how eager housewives were to learn about the solar systems. "Men buy, but women are the users," explains one engineer. "Husbands leave early in the morning and return at night. So housewives need to know about the health risks of batteries, short circuits, and indoor smoke and why there are limits to the daily use of solar power. And what a mother learns, she will teach her children."

Children, however, can also teach their parents, which is why women engineers conduct courses in renewable energy technologies in village schools. They enjoy sharing their knowledge of engineering science and explaining its practical applications in ways young students can understand. "I also invite the teachers to come to my classes," says a GTC engineer. "There is a section on solar technology in the high school textbooks and teachers welcome the chance to hear me explain it. But what surprises everyone most is that solar technology is so simple. I get similar responses when talking about improved stoves and biogas cookers. So when I ask the children if their kitchens at home are full of smoke when their mothers cook, they delight in hearing about improved combustion efficiency and biogas technology. Then they go home and teach their parents what they have learned."

Women engineers see a bigger picture than just their job and the company they work for. They are interested in community life and take time to talk to young students and their mothers. They engage teachers' support for the school program and invite everyone to participate in their solar demonstrations. "Our young people leave the village for education and a job, but you bring knowledge and jobs to us," villagers tell the engineers. Grameen Technology Centers have become part of the village not only by virtue of their name. People see them as benefitting village life.

In future, Grameen Shakti's technology centers will be at the front of the company's organizational development. They will bring down the cost of products and services and lay the foundation for growth for a market that will absorb millions of solar systems, cooking stoves, and biogas plants. They will rely on women engineers for managing production and for the task of turning school dropouts into independent energy entrepreneurs.

True, only a few hundred of these small entrepreneurs in 2010 earned enough to feed a family. But it's a start. Customers trust their expertise, and branch engineers are relieved that they can share their growing workload with energy entrepreneurs. The production and repair centers keep branches supplied with electronic equipment and prepare the company for major growth. No doubt, much lies ahead for Shakti's technology centers.

Grameen Technology Center engineers in Rajshahi

Part Three

Much Lies Ahead

Beyond 2011

Farmer with sickle

7

Change Reaches the Village

While pioneering rural electrification, Shakti followed its own path. It explored uncharted terrain, pioneered a new business model, trained its own staff, and achieved sustainability. Visitors came to learn; new companies entered the solar market. The World Bank encouraged the replication of Shakti's approach.

It seemed as though villages in Bangladesh abounded in opportunities for solar business. As early as 1996, Shakti estimated that the Bangladesh market could absorb 2 million solar home systems. This estimate will soon be surpassed, and the market for cooking stoves may grow even faster. So, the future seems bright for millions of villages, where only fifteen years earlier there were no solar lamps to light up the darkness. Nor did it seem this would change.

Life seems to change slowly in the villages. Farmers plough with oxen. They sow and weed their crops by hand and harvest their rice with sickles, as generations have done before them. Although travel conditions on main thoroughfares are gradually improving, back roads in remote areas remain as poor as ever and the promise of lucrative jobs and better education continues to lure young villagers away to large cities and foreign countries. Innovation and progress seem to happen elsewhere. New business grows in places where it finds what it needs: energy and transportation, information and communication, skills and services.

And yet, change happens in unexpected ways. When Shakti began operations in 1996, mobile phones in villages were almost nonexistent. Today, all of Bangladesh's 80,000 villages enjoy telephone services. A generation ago, microcredit for the poor in rural Bangladesh was unheard of. By 2010, Grameen Bank alone had 8 million borrowers, and many other microcredit organizations were serving the rural population. Remarkably, change does reach the village, induced by innovation and the vision to solve social problems in a business way. And electricity is accelerating the process.

A World Bank study in Bangladesh found that having access to electricity impacted rural households significantly. It increased household incomes by as much as 20 percent, resulting in a corresponding drop of the poverty rate of about 15 percent. Findings also showed that study time for schoolchildren was up to 33 percent higher for those whose homes have electricity. As in the rest of the developing world, many problems in rural Bangladesh are rooted in an energy problem. Providing villagers with even modest amounts of electricity is impacting most every facet of village life.

A Shakti manager with years of experience describes his perception of change in the village: "I can see houses with tin roofs instead of thatched roofs everywhere. That's the most visible sign of change, because villagers can afford them. I see the same thing happening when so many more people can buy a solar system compared to the early days of Shakti. Now village houses light up at night and people talk to their families abroad on their mobile. Customers talk to me about their children's health and progress in school; they ask how they can upgrade their solar systems to improve business. A decade ago, that's what we were telling them."

Attitudes are shifting. Shakti had to overcome resistance when explaining the harmful effects of kerosene lamps and smoke-filled kitchens on family health, but it succeeded. It designed a credit model to make solar power affordable; it created ways for villagers to increase their incomes. Shakti is in the business of social innovation and change. *Solar Power—Better Life—Better Income* is its motto, and bringing positive change to the village, its business.

Beyond Solar Home Systems

Up to now, the majority of Shakti's customers have required only a modest supply of electricity per day. Solar home systems can accommodate private households and small businesses, but medium-sized businesses are more demanding, as are clinics, schools, and mosques. Demand for reliable power will increase in future as information and communication technologies (ICT) become available in rural communities. Some need electricity twenty-four hours a day, seven days a week; microfinance institutions and most other rural services require reliable power as well.

"To compensate for Bangladesh's unreliable power supply," comments a businessman, "I have to build back-office systems that can work on a few hours of power a day. Our technicians must closely monitor voltage when their computers are running and keep a diesel generator on hand in case of power failure." As new technologies are developed to serve the rural population, access to reliable power will be as important as the technology itself.

More immediate concerns for Shakti are its customer demands for fans, irrigation pumps, water purifiers, refrigerators and ice machines to preserve a fisherman's catch. Can these demands be met by small stand-alone solar systems? Or will larger island systems and village networks prove more effective? Biogas plants already produce more electricity than their owners can consume, and micro-utilities serve small-scale networks. In future they could interconnect as hybrid systems and extend their networks to form village utilities to serve entire communities.

Hybrid systems are good prospects for rural business because they exploit naturally given energy resources like solar, hydro, wind, and biomass in clever combination. They can work off-grid in island mode as well as in grid-connected mode. This flexibility allows hybrid systems to be established as needed, large or small-scale, and stepwise extended—ideal for Shakti's rural customers, who want to upgrade their systems when they can afford it. Adaptable technologies are all the more important for Shakti's future expansion, since the rural energy evolution will not follow a master plan, but rather the plans of many diverse users.

Generation, storage, and distribution of electricity from renewable energy sources are hot topics of research and development worldwide. Any breakthrough could fundamentally change the scene for Shakti's business: for instance portable biogas plants made of fiber-glass, which can be mass produced; new light-weight, portable batteries, or windmills which can perform well at the predominately low wind-speeds in Bangladesh. Shakti closely monitors innovation and experiments with technologies.

New solutions for a rural clientele take time to mature, however. The development of low-tech biogas plants has taken years and is still underway. Whatever the technical innovation Shakti offers its village customers, they must be given time to voice their demands and complaints. And Shakti's engineers must adapt generic solutions to specific rural needs as Shakti moves beyond solar home systems.

New Applications

Mobile telephony spread with the speed of an avalanche through rural Bangladesh. Where there were no landlines and expensive phones were beyond reach for the rural population, there are now thousands of mobile phone shops where villagers can make cheap calls. Even in off-grid communities, handsets and solar-powered mobile phone chargers enable locals to connect to family members in Dhaka, Kuwait City, Dubai, and London. Farmers no longer depend on unreliable traders for market information and pricing. They use their phones. Small businesses can shop around for supplies; laborers looking for work are informed by phone when a job is available. In only six years, cell phones revolutionized communication to the benefit of millions of villagers.

IT experts were confident that Internet connectivity would be the next technological breakthrough to reach the villages. Shakti's management, too, hoped the Internet could bring much-needed services to the village and set up an Internet-connected training center on Maheshkhali Island in the Bay of Bengal in 2001. The idea was to provide computer training, since computer-proficient students had much better chances of getting a good job. But from the beginning, the program faced serious obstacles. Provider services and satellite connections were costly; IT personnel had to be hired from the mainland, and they demanded high salaries to work on an island. The center was not sustainable and was eventually closed.

Today, the situation has changed. Enhanced Data Rates for GSM Evolution (EDGE), a technology for wireless Internet access at near broadband speed, reaches 99 percent of all villages and more powerful technologies like Worldwide Interoperability for Microwave Access (WiMAX), are being deployed. If designed to benefit a village clientele, wireless Internet access can serve all levels of the rural population, even the poor.

How this can be achieved was described earlier when the Grameen Bank launched its mobile phone program in 1997. A Grameen borrower received a loan to buy a mobile phone (handset, antenna, battery, and bulk airtime), and let other villagers use the phone for a fee. At the start of the program when demand was greatest, village telephone ladies made a net monthly profit averaging 4,000 Taka (US$100) per month. By 2006, when the program peaked, nearly 300,000 telephone ladies were in business, many of them Shakti customers in off-grid villages.

Later, when one in every four people owned a cell phone and all solar home systems were equipped with mobile phone chargers, the village telephone business lost its momentum. But business can come to life again, this time based on Internet services. The Internet in Bangladesh is still in its infancy: for example, less than 1 percent of the population uses Facebook, leaving plenty of room for business growth and entrepreneurs. Though still rare in rural areas, Internet services are in demand among villagers who enjoy sending e-mails and photos to family members abroad. Journalists send their articles from distant communities to Dhaka newspapers. And since all universities use the Internet, students can download exam results and use Internet-based coaching services.

If cheap Internet access is made widely available to the rural population, the chances are it will spread with the speed of mobile telephony. But remember, when mobile telephony spread through the villages, it was based on Global System for Mobile (GSM), a widely used and mature technology, but not the latest state of the art. What counted as much as the technology was its application: villagers saved wasted journeys to the market and got a good price for their goods. Village telephone ladies and their customers benefitted from mobile communication services and most likely will benefit again from Internet services for education, banking, insurance, and medicine.

Change is underway, reaching the villages and reaching Shakti—change that affects every facet of the company, its market, and its environment. Shakti's business has arrived at a crossroads. The pioneers have done their job, have opened a market. The company cultivated this market with care and reached solid ground. Business development now enters the next stage as Shakti gears up for major growth, for a quantum leap. Again, it won't be able to follow beaten paths. Shakti will have to reinvent itself while preserving its mission and values. Unexplored terrain and an exciting stretch of road lie ahead.

Stove to go

8

A Quantum Leap in Social Business

From Thousands to Millions of Customers

Shakti plans to grow production, sales, and services throughout Bangladesh and expects to expand its solar and stove business from thousands to millions by 2015.

Table 20. Planned Product Installations in 2015

Product Type	Installations (Cumulative)
Solar Home Systems	5 Million
Improved Cooking Stoves	5 Million
Biogas Plants	205,000

Never before has Shakti set such ambitious goals and taken such risks. Why now? To be sure, Shakti is not just out for profit. It does not have to satisfy shareholders, nor does it pay dividends. It reinvests its entire surplus in order to grow and improve the company. What drives Grameen Shakti is its mission to solve a social problem,

In 1996, this problem was clear enough: an estimated 90 percent of rural households were deprived of electricity. Because this is still a problem, Shakti is still on target. Now it will grow by an order of magnitude and face challenges galore in the process.

If one technician can maintain a hundred solar systems a month, 50,000 technicians will be needed to maintain 5 million solar home systems—a daunting prospect. Add the staff required for millions of improved cooking stoves and for biogas plants. About 100,000 jobs altogether will be needed. Such jobs would be more than welcome in any rural area. But how would this job-machine work? Assume further, a solar system costs US$250 and 2 million systems are bought on credit: the credit volume amounts to half a billion dollars. Where would the needed capital come from? These are tough issues indeed, but not all of them entirely new: Grameen Bank already provides credit large-scale to 8 million clients scattered over 80,000 villages.

Shakti prepares for stepping up its business, and the past sections have illustrated how it goes about it. Computerization will play a major role. The branch-network continues to evolve. Branches specialize in specific products and technologies and turn into profit centers. Production goes to the village, and procurement has been redesigned. Shakti's training capacity expands through its Grameen Technology Centers, corps of engineers, and training institutes. Shakti may partner with other organizations to strengthen research and development, production, and sales. Joint ventures to produce hundreds of thousands of solar panels in Bangladesh are well within reach.

And still, the immense challenge of increasing village incomes to spur economic growth remains. With Shakti's support, a recently introduced entrepreneurs' program by the Grameen Bank is opening up new opportunities for rural business. The bank actually introduced the program to solve a local problem. With the help of its higher education loan, 52,000 children from its borrowers' families are enrolled in colleges and universities or have completed their studies with a higher education degree. The problem is that jobs are scarce in Bangladesh. Many graduates have earned degrees in medicine, chemistry, or the social sciences but can't find a job. About 2,000 of them have now taken a Grameen Bank loan to become entrepreneurs.

Rakibul, for instance, graduated with a master's degree in chemistry but couldn't find a job. He took an entrepreneur's loan for 100,000 Taka to start a garment business in Gazipur, repaid the loan, and applied for a second loan for 200,000 Taka. He now has a staff of six and is earning 20,000 Taka per month. Rakibul didn't start from scratch, however. He expanded the small business of his mother, who started her business years ago with a Grameen Bank loan

Young Grameen entrepreneurs are running fisheries, dairy and poultry farms, banana plantations, rice mills, tutoring centers or are breeding tropical birds. Some have started businesses still uncommon in rural areas such as digital photography studios, computer training centers, and e-mail and communication services. Many of these students and graduates may become IT entrepreneurs, expand their mothers' phone business or launch their own IT businesses.

All of these rural businesses depend on electricity. All of them generate increased income for their owners and staff. But of equal importance to Shakti during major expansion are energy entrepreneurs to grow the market. In 2010, Shakti supported forty-three participants in the Grameen program to get started as energy entrepreneurs. They received improved cooking stoves as a loan-in-kind, sold them with a mark-up, and repaid the loans. During the first year, 422 stoves were installed. With Shakti's training and technical backup, this program will evolve and expand to all parts of the country.

Putting the Clean Development Mechanism to Use

Finally, a new instrument, the Clean Development Mechanism (CDM), could boost the energy business. Launched in the context of the Kyoto Protocol (IPPC), the CDM recommends steps to prevent dangerous climate change and assists developing countries in achieving sustainable development. Every improved cooking stove Shakti installs could thus become an instrument of the Clean Development Mechanism.

How chulas, the traditional cooking stoves, waste heat was described earlier. To cook a meal, an improved stove needs about half the firewood of a chula. It emits less carbon dioxide into the atmosphere and spares the dwindling forests of Bangladesh. The millions of chulas Bangladeshis use daily endanger even the Sundarbans, the world-famous mangrove forest and habitat of the Bengal tiger and other endangered species. Improved cooking stoves would benefit the world's atmosphere and the country's nature and ecology.

For this reason, Shakti took interest in the Clean Development Mechanism in 2005. CDM, however, was designed to work well only for big carbon producers or savers like power plants. It would not work on a small scale, e.g., for someone who replaced a chula with an improved cooking stove, thus saving only microscopic amounts of carbon. To measure and reimburse the individual carbon savings made by millions of stove owners would be out of the question. New ways had to be found to honor the effects achieved by deploying great numbers of small carbon emission savers like improved stoves or solar systems.

In 2009, a U.S. specialist and trader of carbon emission rights analyzed the carbon savings resulting from Shakti's efforts in rural Bangladesh. The company found that the yearly carbon-dioxide savings of 200,000 improved cooking stoves were worth US$3.5 million and expressed interest in buying the related emission rights. Shakti's target of 5 million improved stoves could thus yield about a US$100 million.

As a CDM registered project, Shakti's improved cooking stove program can help generate the financial support needed to install 5 million stoves by 2015. Data regarding Shakti's solar home system and biogas programs can be found in the Appendix, in Table 33. Both programs are in the process of being certified.

The CDM money is a welcome new financing option to expand the rural energy market. It is not the only option, however. So far, Shakti's financial scope has been limited; it could not accommodate investors nor access the capital market. This has changed. Shakti has transformed itself into a new kind of organization.

Grameen Shakti Social Business

Since Grameen Bank was founded to provide microcredit to the rural poor, more than fifty Grameen businesses have been established to address the problem of poverty in a sustainable way. Each was created with its own business plan, organizational form, mission statement, and financial structure. Each was dedicated to addressing a different social problem. Grameen Shakti was set up as a company limited by guarantee to supply renewable energy at affordable cost to the rural population.

Grameen Shakti has now a daughter company—Grameen Shakti Social Business (GSSB). Grameen Shakti and Grameen Shakti Social Business are parallel organizations. Grameen Shakti's founder, Professor Muhammad Yunus, explains his motivation as well as the nature and effects of this change. The Chairman of the Board of Grameen Shakti and GSSB, and founder of the Grameen Bank answered a series of questions posed in interviews between January and March 2011 in Dhaka.

Q   Why did Shakti need a new organization?
A   When we created Shakti, we did the only thing we knew how to do: we created a *company limited by guarantee*. But like a nongovernmental organiza-

tion (NGO), Shakti had no owners or shareholders. It was the best legal framework we could think of at the time.

In the meantime, Shakti grew into a big organization, but it didn't fit into my idea of a social business. In spirit I had created Shakti like a social business, but its legal format didn't fit. A non-profit could make a profit, but it could also lose money, no one would blame it; or even notice if Shakti operates as a charity. Shakti could take grants and even distribute all solar panels for free. But this didn't fit into my thinking, because a business must be self-sustaining.

Gradually I tried to refine my idea of a business which works for people and for solving problems, rather than making money out of it. But the only legal framework we had for such a business was a for-profit company. There are only two legal options: one, a company without any owner and second, a company with owners. I saw that the second option fits the *social business* concept without any problem. Social business will be a for-profit business in which the owners declare upfront they cannot take dividends. They only get their investment money back over a specific period of time. This can be defined in the charter.

A social business is thus defined as a non-loss, non-dividend company for solving a social problem. And it must be sustainable; otherwise it will have to shut down. This was my problem when Shakti got so big. A non-profit doesn't have to be sustainable. It can lose money and still continue. So I solved the problem by creating a social business, Grameen Shakti Social Business, to be owned by Grameen Shakti. So now we have an owner.

Q   So you have an old and a new legal format. How does this work?
A   Grameen Shakti Social Business (GSSB) is in the process of taking over from Grameen Shakti all the ground level activities of marketing and maintenance. We thought why not hand over all operational activities and assets of the old company, Grameen Shakti, to Grameen Shakti Social Business. Then this becomes a true social business. We even put social business into the very name of the company. Now we have a perfect fit.

Grameen Shakti (Shakti) is the owner and has kept its name in the new company. It will do supervision, training, monitoring and evaluation. It will also do research and develop new companies. That's its purpose.

At the board meeting, the board will check the progress made on what problem we wanted to solve. Previously, we didn't do this. We were not precise about what impact we wanted to make. Now the board will say: you have a problem to solve. What did you achieve and what is your plan for the future?

Q   What happens to the profits?
A   As a social business, Grameen Shakti Social Business does not give profits to anyone. Its board decides how profits are invested. But don't forget, GSSB is 100 percent owned by Shakti, so the voice of the old company is still there, because it is on the board. It makes sure Grameen Shakti Social Business is the operating wing of Shakti, designed according to the social business principles as we have defined them. And that means the goal of GSSB is to solve social problems, not to maximize profit. If it makes a profit, this is recycled into the company to expand or improve operations. GSSB is doing this; it invests its profit in expansion and improving the company. So it fits into the definition any social business must fulfill.

Q   Why didn't you do this earlier?
A   My concept of social business was not developed properly at the time when Shakti was created. For a long time I thought as long as I don't take profit, it's okay. All of the Grameen companies are legally under the same law – all are non-profits, like Grameen Trust. Then I realized this puts limits on the company. Social business is created to express one's selflessness. If there is no owner, then how can it be expressed? If there is no ownership involved, we cannot attract investors either.

So the legal form should be of a for-profit company, except owners cannot take profit. The profit stays with the company. Whoever is investing in this company cannot get any return on the investment. This is a new concept. As a social business, you don't have to please your shareholders by generating a personal return on investment. You want to focus completely on your social impact. Social business devotes 100 percent of its profits to solving social problems. This leads to long-term solutions.

By the way, the existing company law in most countries is enough to create a social business. That's the beauty of the concept. The only thing is, it must be specified in the charter that the owners cannot take dividends. They only get back their investment.

Q   What are the advantages of Grameen Shakti Social Business over Shakti?

A   Grameen Shakti Social Business can accept further investments, buy shares, invest in the stock market and can have many partners. It can absorb equity from investors; do joint ventures – just like any other company in the world. Of course it will also pay taxes like any other company.

But Shakti cannot have an investor; it's like a foundation which can only take donations, it cannot take equity. The advantage is that legally a non-profit can own a for-profit company, in this case Shakti owns Grameen Shakti Social Business.

Another reason I didn't want social business to be a charity organization is that it gives the wrong impression to investors: people think it's not run like a business, there is no long-term planning. But a social business generates income from its business activities; it plans long-term, gets the job done. That's an incentive for social investors.

Q   **Will Grameen Shakti Social Business continue to promote women?**

A   I just had a discussion with the chairman of a large electronics company who is interested in social business. His company produces an excellent charge controller, which women energy entrepreneurs in the villages of Bangladesh could be trained to make. I told him what we would like to have: training for village women technicians and his company logo on the charge controllers the women produce. "If you certify them, if you train the women," I told him," then the charge controllers made by these women entrepreneurs can be easily certified by your company by putting your logo on the products they make. This tells the market that it is as good a product as made by your company."

This is simply outsourcing production to the village women. It puts the village at the top, because the charge controllers produced in the village will be as good as those made by any major electronics company. GSSB will buy the charge controllers from the women energy entrepreneurs who will earn an income. Grameen Technology Centers will support the process. The charge controllers can also be exported from the village to other countries. Why not? It's a quality product with a world famous brand name. It's not done yet, but this is coming.

Q   **You are on your way to 100,000 green jobs?**

A   Yes, we have over 10,000 already. We are thinking of many new things. We are thinking of women to be a kind of cooking stove sales agent—

not an employee of Grameen Shakti Social Business. She can first install a stove in her own house and invite her family, friends and neighbors, and other women to come and see how she cooks on her new concrete stove. It's a natural home demonstration. The improved cooking stove sales agent will get an attractive commission on every stove she sells.

An improved cooking stove sales agent can start by marketing stoves and then expand to other products. She can also market biogas for cooking. If people have cows or chickens, she can explain how biogas works. She works as a free-lance entrepreneur and is paid for the products she sells. She is not a stove sales person employed by GSSB. She is an independent person who works with an improved cooking stove branch. If she sells a biogas plant, the biogas branch is contacted and she gets her commission. The branch is the back-office for these women sales agents.

Q   How are you going to finance the entrepreneurs?

A   She doesn't need to invest any money; she gets what she needs on credit. When she sells a stove she doesn't have to buy it first. She knows she always has credit to sell ten improved stoves. If she sells and pays back two stoves, she gets two more. If she sells three, she collects money for three and pays back. She continues to sell more and more, and collects the commission for each sale.

A sales agents does not have to bring any cash to invest in her business. She takes the product, sells it and then pays back the company.

Q   Will Grameen Technology Centers become manufacturing hubs?

A   We are coming close to this, let me tell you. We have the energy entrepreneurs producing solar accessories, this keeps the branches fully stocked. The entrepreneurs also do some maintenance, the Grameen Technology Centers and the branches keep up the quality.

Another thing we are trying to do is create a village warehouse which will be stocked with cooking stoves, mosquito nets, shoes and other social business products. It is run by an entrepreneur – not by the branch. The job of the entrepreneur is to sell all these products through the free-lance agents.

There are higher level, sub-regional and regional warehouses—all computerized management information systems (MIS), so you know which item is selling more. GSSB becomes the producer. The ultimate goal is to set up a supply chain through a network of entrepreneurs. Eventually everything will be done by entrepreneurs. I am not talking about rich entrepreneurs; they'll mostly be local women and the poor, who can earn as entrepreneurs. Now, we are in the process of developing the system.

Q   What do you see as the main frontiers of innovation?
A   We're looking for a battery at the cutting edge of technology—environment friendly, long lasting, and movable. Maybe we can't have this all in one battery, but it must be environment friendly. Only then will we invest in a battery factory and produce batteries ourselves to bring down the price. Current demand in the company is over 1,000 batteries a day. Battery supply is our immediate concern.

A joint-venture for a solar panel factory will bring down the price of the panel. This should happen soon. 40 percent of the solar system cost is the cost of the solar panel. We can also buy large size imperfect panels and cut them into smaller panels to suit the local demand. This will help reduce the price.

How the price of the systems can be brought down to serve the poor, how the marketing strategy can generate income for village entrepreneurs, these are the challenges for Grameen Shakti Social Business. It must innovate solutions to achieve social impact. This is at the heart of social business.

Q   What was GSSB's main breakthrough?
A   The biggest breakthrough was changing people's mindsets. People did not think that solar had a future in Bangladesh; it's too expensive, people can't afford it. Solar electricity has no meaning in Bangladesh; the grid will be coming anyway. But now people say, yes, solar is a solution. Yes, it can expand. It's not a pilot project, not just two or three hundred houses, but nearly a million solar systems today; at the end of this year a full million. It's possible, and the business is growing. We didn't wait for the grid. We brought our own electricity.

The social impact is enormous; people have electricity in their homes. They can get connected to the world with mobile phone, TV, Internet. Whatever it means in social and economic terms to have electricity, now we have it here in the villages of Bangladesh and this has changed people's attitude. Now people see the benefit and the future in solar power.

This changes the entire perspective of a village which was not connected to the grid. Before, there was nothing to do in the village after dark. Tiny kerosene lamps provided some feeble light inside village homes; outside the house the moon was the only source of light for a few days a month. After sunset, darkness engulfed the entire village. Now it is going to be very different.

Preserving a Heart for the Village

This book is about people and poverty, economy and technology, innovation and progress. It's about responding creatively to change and how rural business can only survive long-term through innovation and entrepreneurship.

It was Shakti's entrepreneurial culture that allowed its positive impact on rural society. It was a culture that responded to a market which started from scratch and grew in unexpected ways. This market will continue to challenge Shakti in future as new technologies, new competitors and new services arise. If it was a challenge to succeed as a young start-up, to sustain this success as the world's largest solar provider in off-grid rural areas may be an even greater challenge.

Shakti chose to address major social problems by confronting them in a business manner. They will not disappear anytime soon. Despite increased migration to urban areas, rapid population growth has made rural Bangladesh more crowded than ever and rural communities remain mired in poverty. And still, Shakti has found ways to tap their market potential and by doing so improve the standards of living for millions of villagers. The characteristics of the company—its strong rural presence, women engineers, small-scale entrepreneurs and a knack for innovations which shape long-term outcomes—will be the elements that insure the future.

This book presents Shakti as an organization which continues to evolve. Its business development is as much a result of its past as it is an attempt to deal with the daily problems of a diverse and changing rural environment. What remains constant is its mission and its heart for the village. This is the core of the new venture: Grameen Shakti Social Business.

An energy entrepreneur teaching her assistants

Appendix

At a stove factory

Business Characteristics of Grameen Shakti

Area of Activities of Grameen Shakti in 2011

The following characteristics and statistics describe Shakti at the end of fiscal year 2010. More current information can be obtained from Shakti's website at www.grameen-shakti.org.

Table 21. Product Installations

Product Installations Since 1996	Quantity
Solar Home Systems (SHS)	539,504
Improved Cooking Stoves (ICS)	214,125
Biogas Plants	15,543
Micro Utilities	10,000

Table 22. Offices and Infrastructure

Offices in 2010	Quantity
Branch Offices	1038
Regional Offices	137
Divisional Offices	14
Grameen Technology Centers	46

Table 23. Market Coverage

Market Coverage in 2010	Quantity
Districts	64 (of 64)
Villages	40,000
Beneficiaries	3.5 million

Table 24. Selected Business Indicators

Miscellaneous Indicators in 2010	Quantity
Employees	8,900
Staff at head office	< 100
Installed power capacity	26 MW
Energy generation per day	130 MWh
SHS installations per month	20,000+
Technicians trained	7,395
Customers trained	208,063
SHS owners	141,101
SHS maintenance agreements	20,708

Table 25. Business Indicators of Divisions in2010

Division	No. of Solar Branches	No. of Biogas Branches	No. of ICS Branches	No. of GTCs	No. of Employees	Recovery Rate (%)
Barisal	66	1	17	6	765	96.00
Bogra	64	2	17	3	734	94.95
Chittagong	46	0	15	3	314	94.03
Comilla	64	1	14	3	679	99.93
Faridpur	52	6	9	2	453	95.74
Feni	59	1	12	3	505	96.88
Habiganj	61	2	15	2	553	96.00
Khulna	61	4	13	6	623	83.23
Mymensingh	68	3	16	3	716	90.88
Patuakhali	62	0	16	4	684	97.48
Rangpur	60	3	17	2	655	96.00
Shariatpur	61	4	13	2	401	97.00
Sylhet	61	2	12	3	574	93.69
Tangail	61	3	15	4	675	95.92

Business Development

The development of Shakti's business is best characterized by the growth of installations of SHS. The markets for biogas plants and ICS have recently started and show great potential, as stated in Shakti's plans.

Shakti became sustainable in 2000, after four years of operation. In 2003, Shakti benefitted from growth funding which strongly advanced its business.

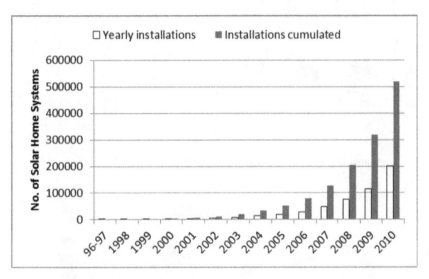

Cumulated Installations of Solar Home Systems, 1996–2010

Table 26. Selected Plans and Goals

Plans for the Year 2015	Quantity
Solar Home Systems installed	5 million
Biogas Plants installed	205,000
Improved Cooking Stoves installed	5 million
Green Jobs created	100,000

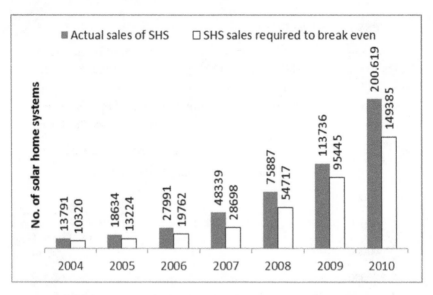

Sustainability of Grameen Shakti, 2004–2010

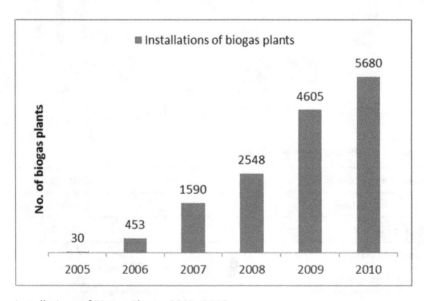

Installations of Biogas Plants, 2005–2010

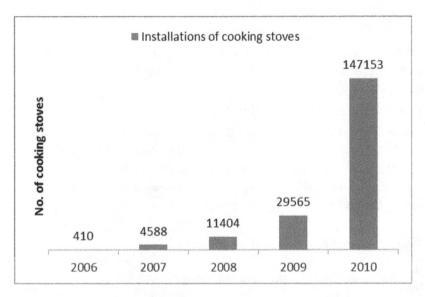

Installations of Improved Cooking Stoves, 2006–2010

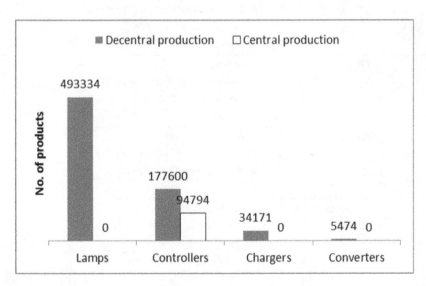

Decentral Production (at GTCs) vs. Central Production in 2010

Products

Shakti markets many versions of solar home systems (SHS), biogas plants, and improved cooking stoves (ICS). Popular product configurations, called packages, are listed here.

SHS Product Packages for Rural and Urban Use

Tables 27 and 28 lists Solar Home System Packages for rural and for urban use. Package price also includes installation, switchboard, and mounting rack.

The small-scale systems (numbered 10 and 11 in table 27) have been on the market for a relatively short time. They enjoy broad acceptance, in particular, by the poorer part of the rural population..

Table 27. Product Packages for Rural Use 2010

SL. No.	No.	Load	No.	Product Package	Package Price (Taka)
1	11	7W Lamp	1	130Wp Solar Module,	65,400
	1	17"-20" B/W TV	2	100 Ah Industrial Battery (Tab. Plate),	
			1	15 Amps Charge Controller,	
			11	7W Lamp,	
2	10	7W Lamp	1	120Wp Solar Module,	62,900
	1	17"-20" B/W TV	2	100 Ah Industrial Battery (Tab. Plate),	
			1	15 Amps Charge Controller,	
			10	7W Lamp	
3	8	7W Lamp	1	85Wp Solar Module,	40,800
	1	17" B/W TV	1	130 Ah Industrial Battery (Tab. Plate),	
			1	10 Amps Charge Controller,	
			8	8 Nos. 7Watt Lamp	
4	7	7W Lamp	1	1 No. 80 Wp Solar Module,	38,400
	1	17" B/W TV	1	1 No. 100 Ah Industrial Battery (Tab. Plate),	
			7	1 No. 10 Amps Charge Controller, 7W Lamp.	
5	6	7W Lamp	1	75Wp Solar Module,	36,900
	1	17" B/W TV	1	100 Ah Industrial Battery (Tab. Plate),	
			1	10 Amps Charge Controller,	
			6	7W Lamp,	
6	5	7W Lamp	1	65Wp Solar Module,	32,800

	1	17" B/W TV	1	100 Ah Industrial Battery (Tab. Plate),	
			1	5 or 10 Amps Charge Controller,	
			5	7W Lamp,	
7	5	7W Lamp	1	60Wp Solar Module,	31,300
	1	17" B/W TV	1	80 Ah Industrial Battery (Tab. Plate),	
			1	5 or 10 Amps Charge Controller,	
			5	7W Lamp,	
8	4	7W Lamp	1	50Wp Solar Module,	26,800
	1	17" B/W TV	1	80 Ah Industrial Battery (Tab. Plate),	
			1	5 or 10 Amps Charge Controller,	
			4	7 Lamp,	
9	3	7W Lamp	1	40Wp Solar Module,	21,400
	1	14" B/W TV	1	55/60 Ah Industrial Battery (Tab. Plate),	
			3	5 or 10 Amps Charge Controller,	
				7Watt Lamp,	
10	2	5Watt CFL Lamp	1	20/21 Wp Solar Module,	11,700
	1	or	1	30 Ah Industrial Battery (Tab.Plate),	
	1	7W Lamp &.	1	5 or 10 Amps Charge Controller,	
		3Watt CFL	2	5W CFL or	
			1	7W Lamp	
			1	3W CFL,	
11	1	5W CFL Lamp or	1	10 Wp Solar Module,	8,800
	2	LED Lamp (18,36)	1	18 Ah Industrial Battery,	
			1	5 or 10 Amps Charge Controller,	
			1	5W CFL or	
			2	LED Lamp,	

Table 28. Product Packages for Urban Use

SL. No.	No.	Load	No.	Product Package	Package Price (Taka)
1	2	20Watt CFL Lamp	2	70/75Wp Solar Module,	75,000
	2	Ceiling Fan	2	60 Ah Industrial Battery,	
			1	400VA pv-Inverter.	
2	3	20Watt CFL Lamp	4	50Wp Solar Module,	105,000
	3	Ceiling Fan	2	100 Ah Industrial Battery,	
			1	600VA pv-Inverter.	
3	4	20Watt CFL Lamp	2	130/135Wp Solar Module,	139,000
	4	Ceiling Fan	2	130 Ah Industrial Battery,	
			1	800VA pv-Inverter.	
4	5	20Watt CFL Lamp	4	85Wp Solar Module,	169,000
	5	Ceiling Fan	4	80 Ah Industrial Battery,	
			1	1000VA pv-Inverter.	
5	2	20Watt CFL Lamp	4	50Wp Solar Module,	111,000
	2	Ceiling Fan	2	100 Ah Industrial Battery,	
	1	21″ Color TV	1	600VA pv-Inverter.	
6	3	20Watt CFL Lamp	4	65Wp Solar Module,	133,000
	3	Ceiling Fan	2	130 Ah Industrial Battery,	
	1	21″ Color TV	1	600VA pv-Inverter.	
7	4	20Watt CFL Lamp	4	85Wp Solar Module,	164,000
	4	Ceiling Fan	2	80 Ah Industrial Battery,	
	1	21″ Color TV	1	1000 pv-Inverter.	
8	5	20Watt CFL Lamp	8	50Wp Solar Module,	199,000
	5	Ceiling Fan &	4	100 Ah Industrial Battery,	
	1	21″ Color TV	1	1 No. 1000VA pv-Inverter.	
9	2	20Watt CFL Lamp	4	65Wp Solar Module,	137,000
	2	2 Nos. Ceiling Fan	2	130 Ah Industrial Battery,	
	1	Computer	1	1000VA pv-Inverter.	
10	2	20Watt CFL Lamp	4	85Wp Solar Module,	166,000
	2	Ceiling Fan,	4	80 Ah Industrial Battery,	
	1	21″ Color TV	1	1000VA pv-Inverter.	
	1	Computer			

Biogas Plants

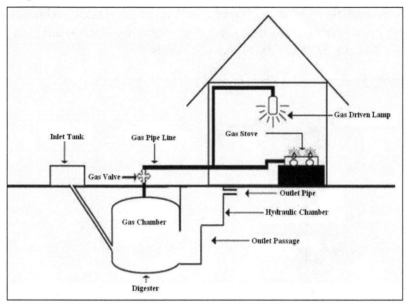

Outline of a biogas plant

Table 29. Characteristics of Biogas Plants

Size (m³)	Usage of Single Burner (hours)	Cow Dung Required (kg/day)	Poultry Droppings Required (kg/day)	Cost (Taka)	Subsidy (Taka)	Down Payment (Taka)	Loan Amount (Taka)
1.6	3-4	43	23	21700	9000	1905	10795
2.0	4-5	54	28	23700	9000	2205	12895
2.4	5-6	65	34	27700	9000	2805	15895
3.2	7-8	87	45	31700	9000	3405	19295
4.8	10-12	130	68	37700	9000	4305	24395

In addition to these standard-size and standard-technology biogas plants, Shakti also installs larger biogas plants (9 or 12 m³), for instance, at large chicken farms. Four small cows are required for a 1.6 m³ plant; thirty cows for a 30 m³ plant. New 1.6 m³ portable biogas plants made of fiberglass are being deployed.

Improved Cooking Stoves (ICS)

ICSs are made from a mixture of cement, sand, and crushed bricks and are set up either on-floor or half-underground. Figure 16 shows a single-mouth, on-floor ICS model. Table 30 lists the common models

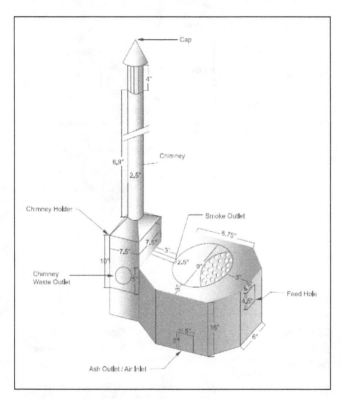

Outline of a single-mouthed cooking stove

Table 30. Price of ICS Models

ICS Model	Prize (Taka)
Single-mouth	760
Double-mouth normal	890
Double-mouth large	1090
Double-mouth commercial	6000

Payment Schemes

Shakti's credit and repayment-schemes are designed to make products afford-able to a rural clientele, which often has little savings and small and irregular income. Shakti's approach to customer financing is characterized by low down payments and extended repayment periods. Such soft financing con-ditions go along with three years of free maintenance of SHS and a five-year warranty for biogas plants.

Table 31. Payment Schemes for Solar Home Systems (2001 – 2010)

Options	Down Payment	Monthly Installments	Service Charge (flat rate)
1	25%	24	4%
2	15%	36	6%
3	100% Cash payment with 4% discount		

Table 32. Other Payment Schemes

Product	Down Payment	Monthly Installments	Service Charge
Micro-utility solar system	10%	36	5%
Small solar system	10%	36	5%
Solar package for urban area	100%	0	*4% discount*
Biogas plant (>4.8m^3)*	25%	12–24	10% of construc-tion cost
Single Mouth ICS	50%	1	0
Double Mouth ICS	50%	1	0
For large family	Cost ca. 1,090 Taka		
Commercial ICS	50%	6	6%

* Shakti offers biogas plants larger than 4.8 m^3. IDCOL subsidizes biogas plants up to 4.8 m^3 with 7,000 Taka per system part of which is paid to Shakti for installation and supervision. This is subject to change.

Carbon Emission Reduction

The carbon emission reductions of Shakti product types have been carefully analyzed. Regional cooking habits have been accounted for, as has the leakage of methane from biogas plants.

The amount of carbon reduction suffices to start small-scale program activities under the UN Clean Development Mechanism (CDM). By the year 2015, Shakti products will increase carbon reductions by about an order of magnitude.

Note that the monetary value of carbon credits (carbon finance) varies due to market conditions.

Table 33. Carbon-Dioxide Emission Reduction Per Product Type

Product Type	Units Installed by 2010	Emission Reduction Per Unit (tCO2/yr)	Emission Reduction Per Product Type (tCO2/yr)	Carbon Finance Equivalent (million US$)
SHS	518,210	0.232	120,224	ca. 1.2
Biogas Plant	14,906	2.08	31,004	ca. 0.3
ICS	192,120	1.04	200,844	ca. 2.0
Total	—	—	**ca. 352,000**	**ca. 3.5**

Initial Training Course for Women Technicians

Several curricula exist for the training of engineers, managers, and technicians. Here is the plan for the initial training of woman technicians.

As production goes rural, the training of local technicians gains in significance. The training is tailored in particular to motivated women in need like school dropouts, widows, and divorcees. Various training courses create the skills to manufacture, repair, install, and maintain all Shakti products. GTCs also teach entrepreneurial skills to freelancing technicians. In future, technology based partner companies will become involved in Shakti's rural production. Table 34 describes an introductory course for woman technicians. Examination is on day 15.

Table 34. Initial Training Curriculum for Women Technicians

Day	Topics of Training
1	What is electricity? How is electricity produced? How can power be transformed into electricity? Types of electricity; Electronics and its many uses; Diode; Transistor
2	Practical on electronic product assembling; Practical on soldering; Practical on SHS accessories and tools assembling
3	Basic electronic technology; Lamp assembling technique; Discussion on SHS
4	Idea about voltage, current, and resistance and their interrelationship; Wire measurement; Ensuring security to electricity usage; Capacitor; Resistance; Integrated circuit; SHS accessories; Solar panel
5	Electrical circuit; Transformer; Electronic module/circuit development; Charge controller: Rules for installing SHS; House wiring; Discussion on electronics
6	Electronic circuit; Short circuit and open circuit; Series and parallel connection; Testing electronic equipment ; Assembling PBC
7	Assembling electronic equipment; Manufacturing and repairing ballasts; Trouble shouting & maintenance of SHS; Identifying problems in charge controllers, ballasts; circuits, etc.; Maintenance of different parts of SHS
8	Manufacturing ballast circuits; Assembling lamp shades; Manufacturing DC-DC inverter circuits; What is biogas? Importance of biogas technology; Benefit of biogas technology; Production cost; Purchase system
9	How to use biogas plants; Precautions for using biogas plants and maintenance of pipes; Use of biogas
10	Manufacturing of charge controllers; Use of slurry; Advantage of using organic fertilizers from biogas; Business potential of organic fertilizers from Biogas
11	Installation of panels: Enough light; Angular installation; Barrier to light by panel tops; Distance between battery and panel; Installation/assembling of charge controller; Installation of battery; Installation of lights; Construction and maintenance of ICS; Familiarizing with conventional and improved stoves; Advantages of ICS and disadvantages of conventional stoves; Learning to construct ICS using conventional methods
12	Wiring; Selecting cables; House wiring methods; Problems related to SHS and testing of different parts; Short circuits; Battery-related problems and their solutions; Steps in installing SHS; House wiring
13	Problems related with lamps; Problems related with charge controllers; Testing charge controllers; Testing invertors; Testing batteries
14	Environment and renewable energy; What is environment? How is environment being endangered? Impact of conventional energy sources on the environment; How is air polluted because of conventional methods of cooking? Ill effects on health; What is renewable energy?

Objectives of Grameen Shakti Social Business

Listed below is a selection of objectives taken from the Memorandum of Association of Grameen Shakti Social Business:

- To acquire, develop, transfer and upgrade technologies in the alternate and renewable energy, energy management, environment and climate changes; energy for health and education; alternative fuels for transport, rural energy, water supply, women in development and related industrial and business spheres through appropriate means including importation.
- To maximize benefit of the society rather than profit maximization.
- To overcome poverty, or one or more problems (such as education, health, technology access, and environment) which threaten people and society; not profit maximization with special emphasis on environment.
- To carry on business with financial and economic sustainability being fully conscious of the environment.
- Investors get back their investment amount only. No dividend is given beyond investment money.

References

Drucker, Peter. (2008). *The Essential Drucker*, New York: Collins Business Essentials

Hammond, Allen, Kramer, William J., Tran, Julia, and Walker, Courtland. (2007). *The Next 4 Billion: Market Size and Business Strategy at the Base of the Pyramid*. Washington, D.C.: World Resources Institute.

Khan, Akbar Ali.(2001). *Discovery of Bangladesh*. Dhaka:The University Press Limited.

Martinot, Eric, Cabraal, A. and Mathur, S. (2001) *World Bank / GEF Solar Home Systems Projects: Experiences and Lessons Learned 1993–2000*. Renewable and Sustainable Energy Reviews 5 (2001) 39–57.

McCraw, Thomas. (2007) *Prophet of Innovation, Joseph Schumpeter and Creative Destruction*, Cambridge: The Belknap Press of Harvard University Press

Van Schendel, Willem. (2010) *A History of Bangladesh*. Cambridge: Cambridge University Press.

Wimmer, Nancy (2008) *Innovations in Rural and Peri-urban Areas*. In: Peter Droege, Ed. *Urban Energy Transition*. Amsterdam: Elsevier

Yunus, Muhammad. (2010) *Building Social Business: The New Kind of Capitalism That Serves Humanity's Most Pressing Needs*. New York: Public Affairs.

Yunus, Muhammad. (1999) *Banker to the Poor: Micro-Lending and the Battle Against World Poverty*. New York: Public Affairs.

Benchikh, Osman and Benallou, Abdelhanine. (1996) *Evaluation of Renewable Energy Potentials and Projects in Bangladesh*. Dhaka: UNESCO

Currency Exchange Rate, Kerosene Price

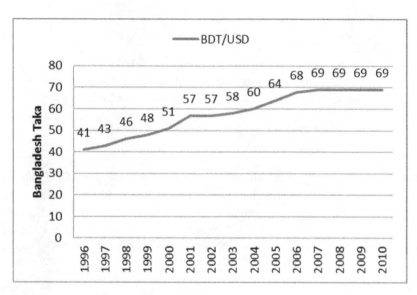

Development of the currency exchange rate

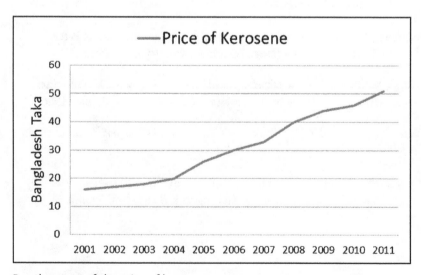

Development of the price of kerosene

Acronyms and Abbreviations

AC	Alternate Current
BDT	Bangladesh Taka
CDM	Clean Development Mechanism
CFL	Compact Fluorescent Lamp
DC	Direct Current
DGIS	Directorate General for International Cooperation (Netherlands)
EDGE	Enhanced Data Rates for GSM Evolution
GSM	Global System for Mobile Communications
GTC	Grameen Technology Center
HO	Head Office
ICS	Improved Cooking Stove
ICT	Information and Communication Technology
IPS	Instant Power System
IDCOL	Infrastructure Development Company Limited
IFC	International Finance Corporation
KfW	KfW Entwicklungsbank
LED	Light Emitting Diode
PPP	Purchasing Power Parity
PV	Photovoltaic / Photovoltaics
SHS	Solar Home System
Tk	Bangladesh Taka
UN	United Nations
US$	US Dollar
USAID	United States Agency for Internat. Development
USD	US Dollar
V	Volt
W	Watt
WB	World Bank / IBRD
WiMAX	Worldwide Interoperability for Microwave Access
Wp	Watt-peak

Index

T

W

Y

About the Author

 Nancy Wimmer is an entrepreneur, researcher, and advisor to the World Council of Renewable Energy. She specializes in microfinance and rural electrification in developing countries. She has been involved with Grameen Bank since 1990 and with Grameen Shakti since its inception in 1996. Her career has many facets. Her political campaigns have targeted the German Government, the European Commission, the World Bank, and the United Nations. Her practical work has led her to the rural parts of Bangladesh, Egypt, El Salvador, India, Honduras, Nepal and Peru. She has lectured and published extensively and has advised investors and entrepreneurs. Nancy, an American citizen, studied law and political science, holds a Masters of Philosophy, and lives with her family near Munich. See her website at www.microsolar.com.